How the Jezebel Spirit Operates and The Anointing that Destroys Her

By

Prophetess Mary J. Ogenaarekhua

Endorsement

Spiritual people sometimes question whether the things they see or experience are related to the Jezebel spirit while some attribute many things to Jezebel and yet, others do not think it exists at all. *How the Jezebel Spirit Operates and the Anointing that Destroys Her* by Prophetess Mary O. provides great clarity about what is and what is not attributable to the Jezebel spirit as she outlines how it operates in different situations and places.

Like so many of Prophetess Mary's books, this book helps open our eyes to how things operate in the spiritual realm and gives us the depth of understanding that we need to navigate a more successful Christian walk. I exhort you to not be afraid of spiritual forces because they exist regardless of whether we go through life with our eyes open or closed. The Lord has already equipped us with mighty weapons of warfare; therefore, this is an excellent opportunity to sharpen your sword.

> "Finally, my brethren, be strong in the Lord, and in the power of his might. Put on the whole armour of God that ye may be able to stand against the wiles of the devil. **For we wrestle not against flesh and blood, but against principalities, against powers, against the rulers of the darkness of this world, against spiritual wickedness in high places.** Wherefore take unto you the whole armour of God, that ye may be able to withstand in the evil day, and having done all, to stand. Stand therefore, having your loins girt about with truth, and having on the breastplate of righteousness; And your feet shod with the preparation of the gospel of peace; Above all, taking the shield of faith, wherewith ye shall be able to quench all the fiery darts of the wicked" **(Ephesians 6:10-16).**

— Lynne Garbinsky, Chief Operations Officer, THGP/MJM, Atlanta, Georgia.

Dedication

I dedicate this book to **God the Father** who sent His beloved Son, **Jesus Christ** to die for my sins, to give me eternal life and to keep me for His heavenly kingdom. I also dedicate it to **God the Son** and **God the Holy Spirit. LORD God, thank You for delivering me from the Jezebel spirit and her evil networks and for using the period in which I wrestled with her and her forces to teach me her ways, her techniques and her evil desires.**

You once said to me concerning the devil; Jezebel's master, **"I will show him how much he must suffer for what he has done to my children."** Thank You for making me one of Your many vessels that You use to make the devil and his agent, Jezebel to suffer. It is an honor to be Your "Battle Axe" against them. Thank You **Lord Jesus** that You are the same yesterday, today and forever; You are still destroying the works of the devil and his agents today. Thanks for using me to continue Your work as it is written:

> **"How God anointed Jesus of Nazareth with the Holy Ghost and with power: who went about doing good, and healing all that were oppressed of the devil; for God was with him"** (Acts 10:38).

Lord Holy Spirit, You have seen me through some of the darkest places that any human being can ever go through and You have brought me out safely each time; even when it meant manifesting Yourself in the physical to do it! You are truly amazing and yes, You are powerful! I truly stand in awe of You **LORD God**. You gave me the words to write in this book and I thank You for also giving me the grace to do it as Your Word says:

> **"The Lord gave the word: great was the company of those that published it"** (Psalm 68:11).

How the Jezebel Spirit Operates and The Anointing that Destroys Her

Unless otherwise indicated, all scriptures are quoted from the King James and the New International Versions of the Bible.

Published by: **To His Glory Publishing Company, Inc.**
463 Dogwood Drive, NW
Lilburn, GA 30047
(770) 458-7947
www.tohisglorypublishing.com

This Book is available at:
Amazon.com, BarnesandNoble.com, Booksamillion.com, UK, EU, Canada, Australia, etc.

Also, see the **Order Form** at the back of this book or call/ email below to order this book.

(770) 458-7947
www.tohisglorypublishing.com
Email: tohisglorypublishing@yahoo.com

ISBN: 978-0-9854992-6-6

Table of Contents

Preface

This book is intended to give the reader a detailed understanding of who the Jezebel spirit is, what she does and how she operates. It will teach you about her origin, her tactics (through men and women) and how to arm yourself against her. Many people wrestle with this spirit in their workplaces, in their homes, in their marriages and in their inter-personal relationships.

Besides the spirits of sicknesses and death, Jezebel is the devil's next most effective agent against humanity. She has brought many down in disgrace, despair, demotion and death! She ensnares those who go after her without being adequately prepared. As you read this book, you will learn how to effectively discern and expel her without falling into her traps.

My desire is that after reading this book, you will have an in-depth knowledge of the Jezebel spirit and you will begin to reclaim the territories that she has stolen from you and the generations before you. This is a must read book for every Christian who wants to walk victoriously against the Jezebel spirit.

— Dr. Mary J. Ogenaarekhua

Acknowledgements

First, I acknowledge You, **God the Father** for being my **Teacher** and for helping me to rise up and write what You showed me about the Jezebel spirit. Thanks for Your grace and for Your patience with me in the times when I was slow to get what You were showing or saying to me. May this book bring You much glory as your children begin to root out the Jezebel spirit and her assignments against them.

I want to thank all those who shared their struggles against this spirit with me. Your struggles encouraged me to teach and to write about this particular spirit. **The Lord Jesus has given us the authority to destroy her and her works.**

As always, thank you Lynne Garbinsky for the many hours that you spent in formatting, laying out and proofreading this book. You are a steadfast soldier and may the Lord bless you beyond your imagination.

Chapter 1
Origin of the Jezebel Spirit

About the Jezebel Spirit

<u>The spirit</u> that we refer to as the **Jezebel Spirit** began its operation against God's plan **in the Garden of Eden.** This spirit is very subtle and it is cruel, vengeful, malicious, impious and crafty. **It seeks to overthrow God's plans on earth and it spares nothing in its attempt to annihilate God's people; especially the prophets. Its goal is to stamp out the Word of God, the institutions of God; including marriage and to put a stop to the worship of the One True God.**

The Woman Named Jezebel

The evil spirit that we refer to as the Jezebel spirit was not given its current name until it used the wife of King Ahab of Israel (Queen Jezebel) to persecute and to kill many of God's prophets and people. Queen Jezebel was the daughter of Ethbaal, the king of the Zidonians (Phoenicians). According to the genealogies given by Flavius Josephus and other classical sources, she was the **great-aunt of Dido, the Queen of Carthage** (founder of modern day Tunisia). She and her husband King Ahab ruled northern Israel in the 9th century; they reigned from 874–853 BC.

Generally, she was regarded as an evil scheming woman and as an **adulteress,** a **prostitute** and **one who promoted the institutions of orgies** and **court prostitution in her Baal worship rituals. As a result of having given herself totally to the workings of this evil spirit in her lifetime, <u>her name has become synonymous with the name of the evil spirit</u>.** In other words, today, both the woman Jezebel and the evil spirit that operated through her now bear the same name! For example, in **Revelation 2:20-23, we see the Lord Jesus referring to <u>the evil spirit</u> by this wicked woman's name:**

"Notwithstanding I have a few things against thee, <u>because thou sufferest **that woman Jezebel**, which calleth herself a prophetess</u>, **to teach** and **to seduce** my servants **to commit fornication**, and **to eat things sacrificed unto idols.** *21* And I gave her space to repent of her fornication; and she repented not. *22* **Behold, I will cast her into a bed, and them that commit adultery with her into great tribulation,** except they repent of their deeds. *23* **And I will kill her children with death**; and all the churches shall know that I am he which searcheth the reins and hearts: and I will give unto every one of you according to your works."

The Meaning of Name Jezebel

Jezebel from *"Promptuarii Iconum Insigniorum"*

The name **'Iezabel'** (Jezebel) is of Hebrew origin which suggests **"a lack of character — implying lack of royal sensibilities or of morality, being unmarried and engaging in adultery or fornication.** In the case of King Ahab's wife, it means someone that is **"not exalted,"** someone that **God does not want to lift up** and someone who is **"abased."** As you can see from the **medal** above, the name **Iezabel** **(Jezebel)** is the actual name of a regent **evil queen in Israel** as stated in 1 Kings 16:31.

Some books refer to her as a **"painted lady"** that was **condemned by God.** This reference to her as a **"painted lady"** was because when the <u>Captain of Israel's army came to her house to destroy her,</u> **she painted her face** in her attempt to seduce him. Painting her face was part of her many scheming and seductive devices to make men fall under her spell. We will address her influence on King Ahab in a chapter devoted to them in this book.

According to Wikipedia, *"the name **Jezebel** came to be associated with false prophets and by the early 20th century was further associated with fallen or abandoned women... **a comparison to Jezebel suggested that a person was a pagan or an apostate masquerading as a servant of God.** With manipulation or seduction, she misled the saints of God into the sins of idolatry and sexual immorality. In particular, **Jezebel** has come to be associated with promiscuity. In modern usage, the name of Jezebel is sometimes used as a synonym for sexually promiscuous and sometimes controlling women."*

The Jezebel Spirit and Adam in the Garden of Eden

The **Jezebel spirit** has been around since the devil unleashed it against Adam in the Garden of Eden and as I just showed you, it took on the name Jezebel because the woman named Jezebel (King Ahab's wife) best exemplified her; she brought the working of the spirit to a whole new level. **The Jezebel spirit looks for a weakness or a vacuum in leaders and as soon as she sees it, she moves in to fill it.** This was what happened when the serpent came to Eve and found her alone without Adam. The evil spirit (Jezebel spirit) that was in the serpent began to deceive Eve because Adam was not there to cover her and she fell for the lies of the spirit in the serpent.

God made Adam the head of his household and He gave both Adam and Eve a commandment concerning the "two trees in the Garden" and He left them with the hope that they will obey Him. **The problem was that Adam was not in his place of authority when the serpent showed up in**

the garden that God left him in charge of. And as we are going to see from Eve's exchange with the serpent, she did not really take God's commandment to heart. **She could not accurately restate the commandment to the serpent and what this means is that she did not take the time to meditate on God's Word to them so that she can know and remember it — she failed to know God by His WORD!**

Therefore, the serpent was able to **twist God's Word** to her and to seduce her concerning the nature of the fruit from the **"Tree of Knowledge of good and evil."** Just as in the case of anyone that does not know the Word of God, she fell for the devil's lies — **Genesis 3:1-6:**

> "Now the serpent was more subtil than any beast of the field which the LORD God had made. And he said unto the woman, **Yea, hath God said, Ye shall not eat of every tree of the garden?** 2 And the woman said unto the serpent, **We may eat of the fruit of the trees of the garden:** 3 But of the fruit of the tree which is in the midst of the garden, God hath said, Ye shall not eat of it, neither shall ye touch it, lest ye die.
>
> 4 And the serpent said unto the woman, Ye shall not surely die: 5 For God doth know that in the day ye eat thereof, then your eyes shall be opened, and ye shall be as gods, knowing good and evil *(the power of seduction through suggestion).* 6 **And when the woman saw that the tree was good for food, and that it was pleasant to the eyes, and a tree to be desired to make one wise, she took of the fruit thereof,** and did eat and gave also unto her husband with her; and he did eat."

The truth of the matter was that Adam and Eve did not eat the fruit of the **"Tree of Life"** so Eve was vulnerable to the devil's lies. Because of Eve's ignorance of the power of God's Word, she willfully disobeyed God without paying attention to the damnable consequence of death that God told them would result from their disobedience. Her husband, Adam who was the head of the household and the Lord of the whole earth, knew what God said to him about the **"Tree of Knowledge of good and evil."** He also decided to set aside God's Commandment to them and yielded to his wife's request to disobey God. <u>Therefore, we can say that Eve was ignorant of God's Word but Adam was not</u>. This is why the Bible says that Eve was deceived but <u>Adam was not deceived</u> in **1 Timothy 2:14:**

> "**And Adam was not deceived**, but the woman being deceived was in the transgression."

What happened to Adam? The answer is simple; **he was seduced!** How do I know this? **The reason is because when I asked the Lord about how Eve got Adam to eat the fruit in disobedience to His Word, He told me to take a look at Eve's punishment or judgment and it will reveal to me the nature of her crime; she seduced Adam!** Therefore, God punished her with the result of her action — sorrowful conception and painful child birth:

> "Unto the woman he said, **I will greatly multiply thy sorrow and thy conception**; in sorrow thou shalt bring forth children; <u>and thy desire shall be to thy husband</u>, and <u>he shall rule over thee</u>. *And unto Adam he said, Because thou hast <u>hearkened unto the voice of thy wife</u>* (a gross weakness on the part of Adam), *and hast eaten of the tree, of which I commanded thee, saying, Thou shalt not eat of it:* <u>*cursed is the ground for thy sake*</u>; *in sorrow shalt thou eat of it all the days of thy life; 18 Thorns also and thistles shall it bring forth to thee; and thou shalt eat the herb of the field; 19*

In the sweat of thy face shalt thou eat bread, till thou return unto the ground; for out of it wast thou taken: for dust thou art, and unto dust shalt thou return" (Genesis 3:16-19).

God meant for love making between a husband and his wife to be to His glory but in the Garden of Eden, the devil immediately taught Eve how to use sex to seduce as soon as she ate of the fruit. Unsuspecting Adam fell into Eve's seductive and manipulating arms and both she and the devil (her new ally) usurped Adam's authority right away because he lowered himself to obey them. This is why now according to **God's judgment on Eve, she will have to earn Adam's <u>affection and attention</u>; she has to work at it** — *and <u>thy desire shall be to thy husband</u>, and he shall <u>rule over thee</u>..."*

In my book titled, ***Experiencing the Depths of God the Father***, *pages 134-135*, I wrote the following about how God re-subjected Eve back under Adam's authority after the Jezebel spirit used Eve to usurp Adam's authority:

"An Analysis of the Judgments
*God in His righteous judgment abased the serpent, <u>**re-subjected Eve back under Adam's authority**</u> and then judged the ground for Adam's sake. **This is one of the finest judgments displayed by God in scriptures. Adam had allowed his wife to usurp his authority and <u>had become subjected to both Eve and the devil by his single act of obeying his wife Eve rather than correct or rebuke her</u>. God had to correct the new '<u>ungodly authority structure</u>'** between Adam and Eve by placing Eve right back under Adam's authority; hence He said to Eve, '<u>**and thy desire shall be to thy husband, and he shall rule over thee**</u>...'"*

<u>This is why the greatest cry of most women concerning their husbands today is that they do not pay them any or enough</u>

attention. The devil once used the Jezebel spirit through the woman to throw God's pristine garden (the earth) into crisis and the man was also equally responsible as his wife. **We can prevent the devil from doing the same in our personal lives today by taking heed to the Word of God. We must all purpose to eat from the "Tree of Life" because failure to do so still carries the penalty of death.** The following is another excerpt from the book titled, *Experiencing the Depths of God the Father, pages 53-54* in which I wrote about the benefits of feeding from the "Tree of Life:"

> *"Effects of Feeding From the Wrong Tree*
> *"If Adam and Eve had eaten from the 'Tree of Life', they would have lived forever and they would not have fallen because the 'Tree of Life' is the Word of God. The Word of God is the only thing that can keep a person from falling into the devil's trap and as long as you are feeding from it, you are not going to listen to the devil's lies. The Lord Jesus is the ultimate Word of God and He is the 'Tree of Life;' everyone that feeds on Him (His Word) has life and everyone that does not, has no life.*
>
> ***Adam and Eve were not eating from any tree and so the devil saw in them a vacuum and he said to himself, 'I will go and feed them the wrong food because they will not know the difference and neither will they know its devastating effects.'*** *When you are constantly feeding on the Word of God, you will recognize when an error comes to you and you will not go for it. This is why a lot of people are deceived today because they do not know the Word of God so they can easily buy into lies and deceits.*
>
> *Also, there are some individuals out there preaching all types of strange doctrines that sound religious; they sound holy but they are not exactly according to the Word of God. Many of them have teamed up with 'New Age Doctrines' and they use these 'New Age Doctrines' to twist their interpretations*

of the Word of God to suit their purposes. Their words may sound 'noble' and they may 'seem' to have 'good intentions' but when you test them with the Word of God, you will discover that they are doctrines of devils.

This is why we that are Christians are not called to live by somebody else's good intentions or what seems good in our eyes but by the Word of God. Many people have followed some seemingly 'good leaders with good intentions' to their own destructions. Examples of which are Jim Jones and David Koresh. Today, their history represents biblically ignorant people who insist on continuing to eat the fruit of the **'Tree of the Knowledge of good and evil'** *and who continue to sell it to others..."*

Chapter 2
The Jezebel Spirit and Samson

How the Jezebel Spirit Operates Against Leaders

The Jezebel spirit likes to target leaders and in the following chapters we will see why. **We are first going to examine how the Jezebel spirit operated against biblical leaders in Israel before addressing how it works in modern leaders and other members of societies including the Church.** The story of Samson is a very good case study of how the Jezebel spirit can destroy a leader.

The Birth of Samson

Samson was a powerful Judge in Israel and he ruled in the days when Israel had judges instead of kings. Samson's birth was of miraculous origin because his mother was barren and could not conceive a child but an angel came and announced to his mother that she was going to have a baby. The angel also told her that she was to call the child's name Samson because he was going to judge Israel. According to the angel, the child would come into this world sanctified from the womb because God has given him a purpose to help Israel destroy its enemies — **Judges 13:5:**

> "For, lo, thou shalt conceive, and bear a son; and no razor shall come on his head: **for the child shall be a Nazarite unto God from the womb: and he shall begin to deliver Israel out of the hand of the Philistines."**

Samson's Perverse Ways

The problem was that as a young man, Samson lacked discipline when it came to women and he was reckless. He knew God's commandments that the Israelites should not marry women from other cultures and other people groups but because he had no self-discipline, he disregarded God's

Word. In other words, he was to set himself apart (sanctify himself) from all other people but all Samson wanted was foreign women and it seriously grieved his parents.

Samson opened the door for the Jezebel spirit to operate against him because his ways were perverse with total disregard for both his parent's advice and God's required sanctification of the children of Israel. He refused to set himself apart for the Lord and to live by God's precepts. In his self-will, he pursued the very things that God commanded His people, Israel to stay away from. On his wayward journeys, he encountered women that had the Jezebel spirit operating in and through them.

Samson and His Betrothed Wife

There are some women in scriptures that have operated under the influence of the Jezebel spirit. Besides Eve, one of the women of significance in scriptures who was under the influence of the Jezebel spirit is Samson's betrothed wife.

During one of his escapades in the land of the Philistines, he met a lady that appealed to him and he went home to his parents and he demanded that they get the lady for him as his wife. Therefore, the wife that was betrothed to him was not an Israelite woman but a Philistine as we see in **Judges 14:1-3:**

> "**And Samson went down to Timnath, and saw a woman in Timnath of the daughters of the Philistines.** 2 And he came up, and told his father and his mother, and said, **I have seen a woman in Timnath of the daughters of the Philistines: now therefore get her for me to wife.** 3 Then his father and his mother said unto him, **Is there never a woman among the daughters of thy brethren, or among all my people, that thou goest to take a wife of the uncircumcised Philistines?** And Samson said unto his father, **Get her for me; for she pleaseth me well.**"

Samson had a riddle based on an experience that he had when he was going up to his betrothed wife's house from Israel. **In his arrogance, Samson put forth a riddle to the Lords of the Philistine about the experience and the Lords of the Philistines turned to Samson's newly betrothed wife.** They placed a demand on her to betray Samson by finding out the secret of the riddle and to tell it to them. A rational person would have seen the plans of the lords of the Philistines through the ways his betrothed wife was manipulating him and would have taken precaution. Samson was too reckless to realize that there was an assignment against him through her. **Samson's betrothed wife pressed him using seduction, manipulation and tears to the point that Samson told her the riddle and she told it to the Lords of the Philistines** —Judges 14:16-17:

> **"And Samson's wife wept before him, and said, Thou dost but hate me, and lovest me not: thou hast put forth a riddle unto the children of my people, and hast not told it me.** And he said unto her, Behold, I have not told it my father nor my mother, and shall I tell it thee? *17* And she wept before him the seven days, while their feast lasted: **and it came to pass on the seventh day, that he told her, because <u>she lay sore upon him</u>** *(manipulation and seduction)***: and she told the riddle to the children of her people."**

As a result, Samson lost the riddle bet with the Lords of the Philistines and he got angry with them and tore down their city and its gate. In retaliation, the Lords of the Philistines burnt his betrothed wife and her family so that Samson no longer had a wife and he left. Again, a rational person would have learned from this experience about the manipulating ways that the Jezebel spirit influences its agents but not Samson.

Samson and Delilah

The next person that we see the Jezebel spirit operating in against Samson is the woman named Delilah. She was also not a member of the Jewish race; she was another Philistine woman. Delilah was a prostitute and she manipulated Samson to bring him to destruction. **She got him to play around with the anointing upon his life until he lost the anointing.**

When it comes to really protecting what God has placed within us, Samson was almost like Esau. He did not place a significant value on the anointing that God had placed upon his life. Can you image the anointing that God placed upon him and how he could not bring himself to see that he was unique by protecting the anointing? He knew that God had chosen him and given him strength like none other; yet, he used the anointing to toy with Delilah just because he knew that he was so strong that he could pick up a building all by himself.

Today, just like Samson, you can see some people in ministry actually toying around with the anointing upon their lives. **When you watch them, you will see that they are acting reckless because they think that they are invincible but they forget that Samson serves as a warning for people who are anointed and treat the anointing recklessly.** When God goes to judge them, He judges them publically just as He did Samson; He brings them to dishonor in a manner that everyone can see. Thank God that in the place of dishonor, Samson finally came to his senses.

When we analyze Samson's life, we see the Jezebel spirit operating in both his betrothed wife and in Delilah. As in a lot of cases, the spirit used manipulation, seduction and tears in his betrothed wife. Delilah's strategy was manipulation, seduction and **jest**. She got Samson to play around with the anointing that was upon his life until he told her the secret about it and then lost the anointing. Samson knew that the Lords of the Philistines hired Delilah against him but he did not care — **Judges 16:4-5:**

> "And it came to pass afterward, that he (Samson) loved a woman in the valley of Sorek, whose name was Delilah. 5 **And the lords of the Philistines came up unto her, and said unto her, <u>Entice him,</u> and see wherein his great strength lieth, and by what means we may prevail against him, that we may bind him to afflict him: and we will give thee every one of us eleven hundred pieces of silver."**

Delilah's profession as a prostitute was not as lucrative as the amount that she was promised if she could successfully learn the secret of Samson's strength and betray it — <u>eleven hundred pieces of silver</u>! That was a lot of money in those days. She received her price after using all the ways of Jezebel at her disposal to bring Samson down to an object of mockery by the Lords of the Philistines. She threw herself at Samson saying tell me the secret of your strength and three times Samson jokingly told her lies.

This continued to the point that she took her request up to a higher level in **Judges 16:15-19.** As you read the story, you ask yourself the following question, "Did Samson not remember what happened with his betrothed wife and how she betrayed him?" I am pretty sure that he did but he thought that he was invincible and he did not know that he could lose the anointing:

> "And she said unto him, **How canst thou say, I love thee, when thine heart is not with me? thou hast mocked me these three times, and hast not told me wherein thy great strength lieth. 16 <u>And it came to pass, when she pressed him daily with her words, and urged him, so that his soul was vexed unto death;</u>**

17 <u>That he told her all his heart, and said unto her,</u> **There hath not come a razor upon mine head; for I have been a Nazarite unto God from my mother's womb: if I be shaven, then my strength will go from me, and I shall become weak, and be like any other man.** *18* **And when Delilah saw that he had told her all his heart, she sent and called for the lords of the Philistines, saying, Come up this once, for he hath shewed me all his heart. Then the lords of the Philistines came up unto her, and brought money in their hand.**

19 **And she made him sleep upon her knees; and she called for a man, and she caused him to shave off the seven locks of his head;** <u>and she began to afflict him, and his strength went from him.</u>"

In the scripture above, we see how the Jezebel spirit used Delilah to press Samson for days until **"his soul was vexed to death"** and how Samson was brought to nothing before her. In his recklessness, he subjected himself to a prostitute and placed the anointing on his head on her laps. While he was asleep, she called a man to shave off the locks on his head and she then began to afflict him with pain. **The sad commentary of the story according to Judges 16:20-21 was that Samson did not know that the anointing had left him.**

"And she said, The Philistines be upon thee, Samson. **And he awoke out of his sleep,** and said, <u>I will go out as at other times before, and shake myself. And he wist not that the LORD was departed from him.</u> *21* <u>But the Philistines took him,</u> and **put out his eyes,** and <u>brought him down to Gaza,</u> and **bound him with fetters of brass; and he did grind in the prison house.**"

Samson had a problem keeping his eyes off 'strange women' and it cost him his eyes. As a result, we can safely say that

Delilah was the first lady that the Jezebel spirit used to destroy a judge in Israel. Although Samson got his strength back, he still died; the end of him was destruction along with the Philistines. As you can see from the story of Samson, when the Jezebel spirit goes after someone, she is not toying with the person for fun; she is after that person's life and position. When God raises you up, your position will immediately release the Jezebel spirit against you and if you play around with that position and the anointing, then the story of Samson is a warning to you about what happens to those who play with the call and the anointing of God upon their lives. **As a leader, always remember that the Jezebel spirit will try to weary you to get its way so when people begin to demand and nag you nonstop, be bold to rebuke them.** Do not out of shame or pressure yield to this spirit.

Chapter 3
The Jezebel Spirit and King Ahab of Israel

She is Against the Worship of God

In the chapter about the *Origin of the Jezebel Spirit*, I discussed who she is and where she came from. In this chapter, we are going to see how she influenced King Ahab to abandon the worship of Almighty God and how she tried to turn all of northern Israel into a pagan nation. **The Jezebel spirit does not like the Judeo-Christian God and she will go to great lengths to see that God is not worshiped wherever she is given a foothold.** King Ahab chose to depart from the ways of the Living God (the God of Israel) and to follow his own ways. In line with this, he married a woman whose father was the king of Zidon and the priest of the god called Baal.

This king's name is Ethbaal; after his pagan god! This marriage was the 'first time' that a king of Israel entered into an actualized marriage alliance with a heathen princess and the alliance brought with it into Israel, heathenistic ways of life. Just like Samson, King Ahab made this marriage alliance knowing what God's Word said about marrying 'strange women'. <u>By this single action, he brought the Jezebel spirit into the ruling house of northern Israel</u>. **This spirit does not only turn away <u>leaders</u> from the worship of the One True God, she raises up her own false prophets or her own false institutions so that her doctrines can go forth.** The biblical account of King Ahab and his wife, Jezebel is a good example of this as we see in **1 Kings 16:30-33:**

> "**And Ahab the son of Omri did evil in the sight of the LORD <u>above all that were before him.</u>** *31* And it came to pass, as if it had been a light thing for him to walk in the sins of Jeroboam the son of Nebat... **and went and served Baal, and worshipped him.** *32* **And he reared up an altar for Baal in the house of Baal, which he had built in Samaria.** *33* **And Ahab**

made a grove; and <u>Ahab did more to provoke the LORD God of Israel to anger than all the kings of Israel that were before him.</u>"

The reason that King Ahab did more to anger God than all the Kings before him was because his wife, Jezebel stirred him up to do them. Queen Jezebel was an affront to the people and to God but King Ahab allowed her to indulge in her pagan religious practices. **He could not control her or rise up as the true leader, so Jezebel became the power behind the throne.** As it was to be expected, Queen Jezebel converted King Ahab from the worship of the Jewish God to the worship of the Phoenician god, Baal.

She also manipulated King Ahab to allow her to erect and operate temples of Baal throughout northern Israel. Her goal was to make Baal worship the only religion in all of northern Israel. She freely built numerous temples to the <u>god called Baal</u> which the Philistines worshiped and which was against the law of God for any Jew to worship. Also, she saw to it that her version of religion (idolatry + witchcraft) received the same patronage as the royal throne. **The historian named Flavius Josephus** wrote the following concerning King Ahab and Queen Jezebel his wife:

"NOW Ahab the king of Israel dwelt in Samaria, and held the government for twenty-two years; and made no alteration in the conduct of the kings that were his predecessors, **but only in such things as were of his own invention for the worse, and in his most gross wickedness.** He imitated them in their wicked courses, and in their injurious behavior towards God, and more especially he imitated the transgression of Jeroboam;

for he worshipped the heifers that he had made; and he contrived other absurd objects of worship besides those heifers: he also took to wife the daughter of

Ethbaal, king of the Tyrians *(Phoenician ancestors of the Carthage Queen; Dido or Elissa)* **and Sidonians, whose name was Jezebel, of whom he learned to worship her own gods.** <u>This woman was active and bold, and fell into so great a degree of impurity and madness, that she built a temple to the god of the Tyrians,</u>

Which they call Belus, and planted a grove of all sorts of trees; she also appointed priests and false prophets to this god. **The king also himself had many such about him, and so exceeded in madness and wickedness all [the kings] that went before him"** (Jewish Antiquity: Book 8, Chapter 13:1 [316, 317]).

Now you can see from Josephus' historical account that Queen Jezebel is in the history books as well as in the Bible as the representation of all that is evil and anti-Christ. She was attached to her heathen worship and she did not spare any expense or pains in promoting idolatry around her. **As we saw in Chapter 1, the Jezebel spirit has been around since the devil unleashed it against Adam in the Garden of Eden but it took on the name Jezebel because the woman named Jezebel (King Ahab's wife) best exemplified her with her evil ways.**

She Usurps the Authority of Legitimate Leaders

We are now going to see how she usurps the authority of leaders. I once asked the Lord, **"Is it everybody that can be influenced by the Jezebel spirit, male or female?"** He said to me, **"When a leader leaves a vacuum in his or her leadership ability, Jezebel recognizes the vacuum and she immediately seeks to fill it."** She loves to have control so she searches for the **weakness** in a leader's ability to lead and she usurps the authority of weak, indecisive and inept leaders in the workplace. What this says to leaders is that you have to step-up to the plate and be a leader.

As she notices that you are a weak leader, or that you lack effective leadership skills, she will try to usurp your authority using any of her agents around you. One example is the story of a man named Naboth in **1 Kings** and it demonstrates how Queen Jezebel was the power behind the throne in Israel during her husband's reign. King Ahab had what we call today, a vacation home and that vacation home happened to be next door to a man named Naboth. King Ahab wanted to plant a garden in it so that he could look out of his house and take in the view but the problem was that the plot of land next to the King's vacation home was <u>Naboth's inheritance</u>. According to the Jewish law about ownership of properties, you are not supposed to sell your inheritance.

Therefore, when the king approached Naboth several times stating his desire to buy his land, Naboth refused. He told the King that it was his inheritance and according to the law, he could not sell it. <u>One day, King Ahab came home pouting and would not eat and his wife Jezebel asked him what was wrong. He told her about his request to Naboth and how Naboth denied his request to buy his land</u>. Upon seeing the weakness in King Ahab, Jezebel sprang into action and she said to him, **"I will give you Naboth's land"** as we see in **1 Kings 21:4-7:**

> "<u>And Ahab came into his house **heavy and displeased because of the word which Naboth the Jezreelite had spoken to him</u>: for he had said,** I will not give thee the inheritance of my fathers. **And he laid him down upon his bed, and turned away his face, and would eat no bread** (*sulking like a child*). 5 <u>But Jezebel his wife came to him, and said unto him, Why is thy spirit so sad, that thou eatest no bread?</u>
>
> 6 And he said unto her, **Because I spake unto Naboth the Jezreelite, and said unto him, Give**

me thy vineyard for money; or else, if it please
thee, I will give thee another vineyard for it: and
he answered, I will not give thee my vineyard. 7
And Jezebel his wife said unto him, **Dost thou now
govern the kingdom of Israel? arise, and eat bread,
and let thine heart be merry: I will give thee the
vineyard of Naboth the Jezreelite.**"

To carry out her plan of giving Naboth's vineyard to King
Ahab, she usurped both the authority and the power of the
King. **We see her being used by the spirit that bears her
name against Naboth who fears God and against Israel's
leaders in the city where Naboth lived.** According to **1 Kings
21:8-16,** she told the leaders in Naboth's city what to do:

"**So she** *(Jezebel)* **wrote letters in Ahab's name, and
sealed them with his seal, and sent the letters
unto the elders and to the nobles that were in his
city,** dwelling with Naboth. 9 And she wrote in the
letters, saying, Proclaim a fast, and set Naboth on
high among the people: 10 And **set two men, sons of
Belial** *(lairs, amoral men)*, **before him, to bear witness
against him,** saying, Thou didst blaspheme God
and the king. And then carry him out, and stone
him, that he may die.

11 And **the men of his city, even the elders and
the nobles** who were the inhabitants in his city,
**did as Jezebel had sent unto them, and as it was
written in the letters which she had sent unto
them.** 12 They proclaimed a fast, and set Naboth on
high among the people. 13 And there came in two
men, children of Belial, and sat before him: and the
men of Belial witnessed against him, even against
Naboth, in the presence of the people, saying,
Naboth did blaspheme God and the king.

Then they carried him forth out of the city, and stoned him with stones, that he died. *14* **Then they sent to Jezebel, saying Naboth is stoned, and is dead.** *15* And it came to pass, when Jezebel heard that Naboth was stoned, and was dead, that Jezebel said to Ahab, **Arise, take possession of the vineyard of Naboth the Jezreelite, which he refused to give thee for money: for Naboth is not alive, but dead.** *16* And it came to pass, when Ahab heard that Naboth was dead, that Ahab rose up to go down to the vineyard of Naboth the Jezreelite, to take possession of it."

From the above scriptures, it is clear that Ahab was a weak and wicked King because he did not ask Jezebel about what happened to Naboth and his sons or how they all so suddenly died. He was just pleased that Jezebel did what he could not do — get the vineyard. I am pretty sure that he later heard about what happened to Naboth and his sons but he allowed Jezebel to get away with her crime of killing an innocent man and of perverting the elders, the leaders and citizens of one of his cities. It did not bother him that they raised up false witnesses in order to condemn innocent Naboth.

Summary of Ahab's and Jezebel's Relationship

Concerning the relationship between King Ahab and his wife Jezebel, we can say that Queen Jezebel saw a weakness in King Ahab's leadership ability and character. As a result, she declared to him that she would take care of what he could not. We also saw how she dealt with the leaders of the cities under their jurisdiction. During the reign of King Ahab, the appropriate question would be, **who was the leader or King of Israel?** She went behind the scenes and she took control of the affairs of the kingdom by telling the nobles and leaders what to do in various cities. They followed her instructions to the letter; even when she called for the killing of an innocent man and with the leaders' full knowledge that the man was truly innocent.

The Jezebel spirit misuses her power once she gets it and the leaders in Naboth's city were under her spell. **She has a strong need to control leaders and it is one of the reasons why besides using a wife to usurp the position and authority of a weak husband, she seldom bothers herself on the interpersonal level where there is no authority or position of prominence for her and where there is no glory for her to bask in.** Therefore, when someone tells you that they are dealing with the Jezebel spirit, you have to be able to show the person how the spirit operates because some of the things that attract the Jezebel spirit are authority and power.

Chapter 4
The Jezebel Spirit and the Prophet Elijah

She Promotes Her Own Doctrines

The Jezebel spirit has prophets and teachers that help her to advance her religious and social doctrines. To effectively permeate any society with her ungodly doctrines, she systematically attacks God's legally established true religion, moral laws and codes of ethics in a society. After she takes over the authority of a legitimate leader, she then activates her own false prophets to preach and teach her ungodly doctrines in place of God's Word.

The Prophet Elijah and the Prophets of Baal on Mount Carmel

In the days of the Prophet Elijah, Queen Jezebel elevated and crowned Baal worship with royal prestige. According to the words of the Prophet Elijah in **1 Kings 18:18-19, four hundred and fifty false prophets ministered to Baal under her reign, apart from the four hundred false prophets of the groves that ate at her table:**

> "...Ye have forsaken the commandments of the LORD, and thou (King Ahab) hast followed Baalim. 19 Now therefore send, and gather to me all Israel unto Mount Carmel, **and the prophets of Baal four hundred and fifty, and the prophets of the groves four hundred, which eat at Jezebel's table.**"

She had so many prophets of God killed to the point that the citizens of northern Israel were divided in their hearts as to who was the true God: the God of Israel or Baal? Therefore, the Prophet Elijah challenged the false prophets of Baal to a contest on Mount Carmel as recorded in **1 Kings 18:21-24**. He wanted the people of Israel to know

who the real God was and the following is what he said
to the people of Israel at the competition that he set up
between God and Baal:

> **"And Elijah came unto all the people,** and said,
> **How long halt ye between two opinions? if the
> LORD be God, follow him: but if Baal, then
> follow him.** And the people answered him not a
> word. 22 Then said Elijah unto the people, I, even
> I only, remain a prophet of the LORD; but Baal's
> prophets are four hundred and fifty men.

> 23 <u>Let them therefore give us two bullocks; and let
> them choose one bullock for themselves, and cut
> it in pieces, and lay it on wood, and put no fire
> under: and I will dress the other bullock, and lay it
> on wood, and put no fire under:</u> 24 **And call ye on
> the name of your gods, and I will call on the name
> of the LORD: <u>and the God that answereth by fire,
> let him be God</u>.** And all the people answered and
> said, It is well spoken."

**Of course, our God, the God of Israel; the Only One and
True God was the only one that answered by fire!** Thus,
the Prophet Elijah exposed Baal as a false "god" and its false
prophets as powerless. He then had the false prophets killed
that day as stated in **1 Kings 18:40:**

> "And Elijah said unto them, **Take the prophets of
> Baal; let not one of them escape. And they took
> them: and Elijah brought them down to the brook
> Kishon, and slew them there.**"

When Queen Jezebel heard about what the Prophet Elijah
had done, she became his enemy but as an evidence
of his weakness, King Ahab did nothing to protect the
other prophets of God from being killed by his wife. **As a
demonstration of her anger, Jezebel sent a death threat**

to the Prophet Elijah. We see in **1 Kings 19:1-2** below, Jezebel's audacity as she acted as though she was the ruler of Israel and not King Ahab:

> "And <u>Ahab told Jezebel all that Elijah had done</u>, and withal how he had slain all the prophets with the sword. 2 **Then Jezebel sent a messenger unto Elijah, saying, So let the gods do to me, and more also, if I make not thy life as the life of one of them by tomorrow about this time.**"

King Ahab himself went on the hunt for the head of the Prophet Elijah in his attempt to accomplish his wife's decree against the Prophet Elijah. **He searched high and low for the Prophet Elijah in order to kill him.** We can see this in the <u>statement</u> of his trusted servant Obadiah when he met the Prophet Elijah in **1 Kings 18:7-12:**

> "**And as Obadiah was in the way, behold, Elijah met him:** and he knew him, and fell on his face, and said, Art thou that my lord Elijah? 8 And he answered him, <u>I am: go, tell thy lord, Behold, Elijah is here</u>. 9 **And he said, What have I sinned, that thou wouldest deliver thy servant into the hand of Ahab, to slay me?** 10 <u>**As the LORD thy God liveth, there is no nation or kingdom, whither my lord hath not sent to seek thee: and when they said, He is not there; he took an oath of the kingdom and nation, that they found thee not.**</u>

> 11 And now thou sayest, Go, tell thy lord, Behold, Elijah is here. 12 **And it shall come to pass, as soon as I am gone from thee, that the Spirit of the LORD shall carry thee whither I know not; and <u>so when I come and tell Ahab, and he cannot find thee, he shall slay me</u>:** but I thy servant fear the LORD from my youth..."

She Seeks to Silence the Voice of God's People

Her goal is to silence God's voice in the land so that only her followers' voices and doctrines will be heard. This goal of silencing the voices of God's prophets is now being manifested in our society and many societies around the world today. For example, when true Christians say that adultery, fornication, homosexuality, transgender, pornography, etc., are against the Word of God, they are branded as intolerant. Also, they refer to true Christians as people that have some kind of phobia; they make us out to be the bad guys.

On the other hand, those who are preaching heresies about how God does not know what makes a man and a women are allowed and even encouraged to scream their heresies at the general population from every media avenue that they can get their hands on. A lot of TV programs and movies now feel that it is necessary or essential to have gay scenes or series in their attempts to assault and bombard the eyes and minds of their TV viewers! They want to <u>desensitize</u> the general public to the aberrations that the programs represent so that they can embrace them. Any Christian or even none Christian who complains is instantly demonized by the media.

As true children of the Jezebel spirit, those whose lifestyles are contrary to the Word of God want impunity to be and to do whatever they want to do without any righteous voice to hold them accountable to their Creator! They want all the righteous voices silenced. This is one of Jezebel's goals; silencing the voice of God's people. That is why in **1 Kings 18:4,** we learned that to safeguard her evil doctrines and Baal worship, Queen Jezebel killed off many of God's prophets. Some people like Obadiah hid some of God's prophets in caves to keep Jezebel and her agents from killing them:

> **"For it was so, when Jezebel cut off the prophets of the LORD, that Obadiah took an hundred**

prophets, and hid them by fifty in a cave, and fed them with bread and water..."

Jezebel had killed so many of God's prophets to the point that the Prophet Elijah genuinely thought that he was the only one left! To correct the Prophet Elijah's erroneous belief about being the only one left, God told him that there were 7,000 of His prophets that Jezebel could not touch — **1 Kings 19:13-18:**

"And, behold, there came a voice *(God's)* unto him, and said, <u>What doest thou here, Elijah</u>? *(Elijah was hiding)* 14 And he *(Elijah)* said, **I have been very jealous for the LORD God of hosts: because the children of Israel have forsaken thy covenant, thrown down thine altars, and slain thy prophets with the sword; and I, even I only, am left; and they seek my life, to take it away...**18 Yet I *(God)* have left me <u>seven thousand</u> in Israel, all the knees which have not bowed unto Baal, and every mouth which hath not kissed him."

The scriptures above show us how Jezebel declared war against God's prophets in those days and sent out her people to slaughter them thereby prompting God's prophets to go into hiding. God in His mercy hid all of His prophets that did not compromise themselves with Jezebel and Baal worship. We will do well to stay away from this evil spirit and all her ways because it is still in the earth today and it still hates God's prophets and God's people.

She Will Seek the Heads of God's People in the End Time

The Jezebel spirit seeks the head of God's prophets and God's people so, keep your head intact if you have an anointing upon it. **Do not be like Samson who handed his head over to a Jezebel woman. I say this because**

in the time of tribulation, they are going to bring back the guillotine and who do you think is behind it? The Jezebel spirit of course.

During this time, many Christians will go into hiding but not those who had been straddling the fence in their Christian walk and were not fully committed to Christ. They will either get their heads cut off when they eventually take a stand for their Christian faith and refuse to accept the "Mark of the Beast" or they will accept it to save their heads. You can tell that the Jezebel spirit is going to have great influence at that time because she has always wanted the head of God's people. She wanted the head of the Prophet Elijah but she failed to get it. We will examine her hunt for the heads of God's people again as revealed in the New Testament.

She Seeks to Frighten God's Prophets and People

This is the one spirit that can cause <u>some</u> of God's prophets to become fearful and weary. As we saw in the way the spirit moved through Samson's wife and again in Delilah, the Jezebel spirit is unrelentless in her quest; as a result, it can make some people to become weary. **She used Delilah to vex Samson almost to death!** According to the scripture below, the Prophet Elijah was so tired of fighting the Jezebel spirit that he requested God to take him away from the earth. He genuinely feared for his life and as a result, he fled into the wilderness as recorded in **1 Kings 19:3-4:**

> **"And when he saw that, he arose, and went for his life, and came to Beersheba, which belongeth to Judah, and left his servant there.** 4 But he himself went a day's journey into the wilderness, and came and sat down under a juniper tree: and **he requested for himself that he might die; and said, It is enough; now, O LORD, take away my life; for I am not better than my fathers."**

When going after the Jezebel spirit, we are not to be weary and we are not to be afraid of her because God has not given us the spirit of fear — **2 Timothy 1:7:**

> **"For God hath not given us the spirit of fear;** but of power, and of love, and of a sound mind."

We cannot allow the Jezebel spirit to use fear to magnify any situation in our lives so we must stand our ground and overcome her efforts to make us despair or weary.

Chapter 5
The Jezebel Spirit and Queen Athaliah of Israel

Another woman used by the Jezebel spirit in the Old Testament is called **Athaliah. She was the daughter of King Ahab and his wife Jezebel. She is the only woman that single handedly ruled as a Queen in Israel.** Israel was a very male dominated society and women were not even allowed into the sacred sections of the Temple and other places where the men gathered. Therefore, the question is: **how did this woman get to the point of usurping the authority of the heir apparent and all the other heirs to the throne to become queen in those days?**

The Jezebel Spirit is Brought into the Ruling House of David

King Jehoshaphat's son, Jehoram married Queen Jezebel's daughter, Athaliah. Therefore, like her mother, she was the queen during the reign of her husband King Jehoram. They had several children and upon the death of her husband, her son, Ahaziah became king. **As a result, while her brother, Joram was king over northern Israel, her son Ahaziah was King in Judah.** Unfortunately for King Ahaziah, the day that he chose to visit King Joram his uncle; was the very day that Jehu the captain of the northern army of Israel came to execute God's judgment against the house of Ahab —**2 Kings 8:25-29:**

> "**In the twelfth year of Joram the son of Ahab king of Israel did Ahaziah the son of Jehoram king of Judah begin to reign.** 26 Two and twenty years old was Ahaziah when he began to reign; and he reigned one year in Jerusalem. **And his mother's name was Athaliah, the daughter of Omri king of Israel** (*Ahab's father*). 27 **And he walked in the way**

49

of the house of Ahab, and did evil in the sight of the LORD, as did the house of Ahab: for he was the son in law of the house of Ahab.

28 And he went with Joram the son of Ahab to the war against Hazael king of Syria in Ramothgilead; and the Syrians wounded Joram. 29 And king Joram went back to be healed in Jezreel of the wounds which the Syrians had given him at Ramah, when he fought against Hazael king of Syria. **And Ahaziah the son of Jehoram king of Judah went down to see Joram the son of Ahab in Jezreel, because he was sick."**

In other words, King Ahaziah of Judah was visiting his uncle, King Joram of northern Israel (both descendants of King Ahab) when Jehu came to execute God's judgment against the house of Ahab and Jehu killed both of them that day — **2 Kings 9:23-27:**

"And Joram turned his hands, and fled, and said to Ahaziah, There is treachery, O Ahaziah. 24 **And Jehu drew a bow with his full strength, and smote Jehoram between his arms, and the arrow went out at his heart, and he sunk down in his chariot...But when Ahaziah the king of Judah saw this, he fled by the way of the garden house. And Jehu followed after him, and said, Smite him also in the chariot.** And they did so at the going up to Gur, which is by Ibleam. **And he fled to Megiddo, and died there."**

What this means is that Athaliah (King Ahaziah's mother), lost both her brother and her son the king on the same day!

Athaliah Reigns as Queen for Six years

When Athaliah heard that her son the king has been killed, she immediately killed off all the royal seeds (including her own grandchildren) and took over the throne but one of her step-daughters hid one of her little brothers (Joash) as we see in **2 Kings 11:1-3**. Athaliah did not know that there was one child left that can still ascend to the throne so, she took over the throne and began to reign as queen!:

> "**And when Athaliah the mother of Ahaziah saw that her son was dead, she arose and destroyed all the seed royal**. 2 But Jehosheba, the daughter of king Joram, sister of Ahaziah, took Joash the son of Ahaziah, and stole him from among the king's sons which were slain; and they hid him, even him and his nurse, in the bedchamber from Athaliah, so that he was not slain. 3 And he was with her hid in the house of the LORD six years. **And Athaliah did reign over the land**."

Her reign lasted for six years. She was the only woman that single handedly ruled as a queen in Israel and she was the daughter of Queen Jezebel. As you can see, this spirit loves national positions and loves authority. It will do anything to gain power.

Chapter 6
The Jezebel Spirit and King Herod

King Herod Married His Brother's Wife

As revealed in the New Testament, another Queen of Israel that allowed herself to be used by the Jezebel spirit is Herodias, King Herod's wife. In the days of John the Baptist, there was adultery and incest in the royal family. Contrary to the desires of the Jewish people, the Emperor Augustus of Rome and Marc Anthony made the son of a wealthy Jewish man (Herod) king over Judaea. Herod had a brother named Philip and the Emperor Augustus gave him a lesser region to rule over—Macedonia. Therefore, while Herod reigned over Judaea, his brother Philip was king of the Macedonia area. Herodias, King Philip's wife decided that she wanted to be queen over the well-known region of Judaea.

Therefore, she began a love affair with her husband's brother King Herod. She left her husband and married her brother-in-law, King Herod taking her daughter Salome with her. These events took place at the time that John the Baptist's ministry was going on and John condemned both King Herod's and Herodias's immoral and adulterous lifestyle. He told King Herod that being the King does not give him the right to violate God's law concerning his brother's wife—it was not lawful for him to marry his brother's wife. As a result, John the Baptist publicly condemned King Herod's marriage to his brother Phillip's wife and he demanded that they put an end to it. As result, Queen Herodias hated John and had it out for him —**Mark 6:17-19:**

> "For Herod himself had sent forth and **laid hold upon John, and bound him in prison for Herodias' sake, his brother Philip's wife: for he had married her.** 18 **For John had said unto Herod, It is not lawful for thee to have thy brother's wife.** 19 Therefore Herodias had a quarrel against him, and would have killed him; but she could not..."

Now, we are going to see how the **Jezebel spirit** manipulated King Herod to get John the Baptist beheaded. **The Jezebel spirit immediately saw King Herod's weakness concerning his niece Salome; Herodias and his brother Phillip's daughter. He was lusting after her and the Jezebel spirit took advantage of it.** Herodias had witnessed her husband lusting after her young daughter and this provided the Jezebel spirit that was operating through her an opportunity to device a way to get rid of John the Baptist.

Jezebel's Manipulation of King Herod

During King Herod's birthday celebration, Queen Herodias arranged with her daughter to entice and seduce King Herod with a dance so that she can entrap him. When King Herod was spell bound after Salome had danced for Him, she and her mother placed King Herod in a position where he had no choice but to deliver the head of John the Baptist to them on a platter — **he was successfully manipulated with his lust and by the time he realized it, it was too late for him to redeem the situation.** We see the account of the events in **Matthew 14:6-11:**

> "But when Herod's birthday was kept, the daughter of Herodias danced before them, and pleased Herod. *7* **Whereupon he promised with an oath to give her whatsoever she would ask.** *8* **And she, being before instructed of her mother,** said, Give me here John Baptist's head in a charger. *9* And the king was sorry: **nevertheless for the oath's sake, and them which sat with him at meat, he commanded it to be given her.** *10* And he sent, and beheaded John in the prison. *11* **And his head was brought in a charger, and given to the damsel: and she brought it to her mother.**"

To tell us that the Jezebel spirit was at work in the situation, St. Matthew made it a point to let us know that it was **already prearranged** between Salome and her mother about what she was to ask for. They knew that on his own, King Herod regarded John the Baptist as a holy man and would not have dared to raise his hand against John so his wife and step-daughter backed him into a corner with his **own words** and in the presence of dignitaries. As a result, he gave in to their manipulation as we see in **Mark 6:20-26**:

> "For Herod feared John, knowing that he was a just man and an holy, and observed him; and when he heard him, he did many things, and heard him gladly... 26 **And the king was exceeding sorry; yet for his oath's sake** (*his own words*), **and for their sakes which sat with him, he would not reject her.**"

King Herod's lust for Herodias' daughter was a dangerous weakness and the Jezebel spirit exploited it as in any other weak leader; she manipulates leaders to get her way. **This shows us that lust is an effective tool that the Jezebel spirit uses against leaders because what sane king would offer half of his kingdom to a young girl just to get into her pants.** According to their secret plan, she would come in and dance to seduce the king when the king was venerable, she would ask for the head of John the Baptist.

Queen Herodias knew how to get what she wanted; she knew that the King's word would bind him before all his guests and the tool that she used was seduction, sex and manipulation. She got King Herod to do what he would not have agreed to do on his own! You have to watch out for the Jezebel spirit because she is good at manipulation.

John the Baptist Had the Elijah Anointing

The Prophet Elijah escaped with his head from the Jezebel spirit but John the Baptist lost his head to her. **The Jezebel spirit targeted John the Baptist because according to the Lord Jesus in Matthew 11:7-15, John the Baptist had the Elijah Anointing:**

"And as they departed, **Jesus began to say unto the multitudes concerning John,** What went ye out into the wilderness to see? A reed shaken with the wind? *8* But what went ye out for to see? A man clothed in soft raiment? behold, they that wear soft clothing are in kings' houses. *9* But what went ye out for to see? A prophet? yea, I say unto you, and more than a prophet. *10* For this is he, of whom it is written, <u>Behold, I send my messenger before thy face, which shall prepare thy way before thee</u>.

11 Verily I say unto you, <u>Among them that are born of women there hath not risen a greater than John the Baptist</u>: notwithstanding he that is least in the kingdom of heaven is greater than he. *12* And from the days of John the Baptist until now the kingdom of heaven suffereth violence, and the violent take it by force. *13* For all the prophets and the law prophesied until John. *14* **And if ye will receive it, this is Elias** *(Elijah)*, **which was for to come.** *15* He that hath ears to hear, let him hear."

The Lord Jesus quoted **Malachi 4:5-6** in the scripture above. John the Baptist had a very important ministry concerning the family unit (reconciling children with their fathers) and this **moral aspect of John's call** angered the Jezebel spirit:

"**Behold, I will send you Elijah the prophet before the coming of the great and dreadful day of the LORD:** *6* And <u>he shall turn the heart of the fathers to the children, and the heart of the children to their fathers</u>, lest I come and smite the earth with a curse."

The Jezebel spirit regards any voice that preaches righteousness as her enemy. Her solution is to get rid of the voices of the righteous.

Chapter 7
The Jezebel Spirit in the Church

In the New Testament Church, the Jezebel spirit is shown as **a usurper, a seducer, a fornicator, a prophetess, a teacher, a mother** and **an idolater.** This is the reason that you have to be careful as a born again Christian <u>not to fall into her doctrines</u> even within the Church of Jesus Christ. **You also cannot afford to become one of her children or her disciple.** Yes, in the Church, she has children that repeat her evil teachings and her evil doctrines from the pit of hell and some of them are in leadership! The Lord Jesus referred to her in **Revelation 2:18-27** as follows:

"And unto the angel of the church in **Thyatira** write; These things saith the Son of God, who hath his eyes like unto a flame of fire, and his feet are like fine brass; 19 I know thy works, and charity, and service, and faith, and thy patience, and thy works; and the last to be more than the first.

20 **Notwithstanding I have a few things against thee, because thou sufferest that woman Jezebel, which calleth herself a prophetess, <u>to teach</u> and <u>to seduce my servants</u> to commit fornication, and <u>to eat things sacrificed unto idols.</u>** 21 **And I gave her space to repent of her fornication; and she repented not.** 22 **Behold, I will cast her into a bed, <u>and them that commit adultery with her</u> into great tribulation, except they repent of their deeds.**

23 **And I will kill <u>her children</u> with death; and all the churches shall know that I am he which searcheth the reins and hearts**: and I will give unto every one of you according to your works. 24 **But unto you I say, and unto the rest in Thyatira, as many as have not this doctrine, and which have**

not known the depths of Satan, as they speak; I will put upon you none other burden.

25 But that which ye have already hold fast till I come. 26 **And he that overcometh, and keepeth my works unto the end, to him will I give power over the nations:** 27 And he shall rule them with a rod of iron; as the vessels of a potter shall they be broken to shivers: even as I received of my Father."

When given a place in the church, the Jezebel spirit immediately ingratiates herself into the authority sphere of the leader. **She seizes on the weakness or the incompetence of the leader because she comes with "a vast knowledge" of how things are done effectively and she flatters or seduces the leader (whichever one works) to usurp the leader's authority.** In no time, she becomes the mouth piece of the leader and before long, her instructions (doctrines) become the prevalent modus operandi or way of doing things in the church. **Instead of the pastor being the teacher and the prophet of the house, she becomes the teacher with her title of being the prophetess of the house. She then begins to have the Word of the Lord for the church every Sunday!**

She uses her so-called prophetic words to win a lot of the congregation to herself and to control the unsuspecting. **This is why a lot of pastors' spouses or trusted assistants are particularly vulnerable to her.** This is also one of the reasons why in some churches, the pastor's spouses that are prophetesses and teachers are her children because they walk in rebellion to their spouses and they usurp their authority. They may be part of the head of the church but they are influenced by the Jezebel spirit. **Therefore, in the church, you identify the Jezebel spirit by her works.**

As an itinerant preacher, I have been to churches where so-called "prophetesses" used the *"word of the Lord"* to hijack services and in doing so, quenched the anointing that was built up during Praise and Worship while the pastors just sat there and did nothing. In most cases, the pastors allowed them to usurp not only their authority but also to make the entire congregation listen to them for long periods of time while they give the *"word of the Lord"* in their attempts to control certain church members. They usually act very spiritual as they call people out from the congregation to speak the *"word of the Lord"* over them.

Therefore as a pastor, if you have someone (male or female) in your congregation who hijacks your service on Sundays with the *"word of the Lord"* and who uses it to show how spiritual he or she is, make them sit down. Do not give him or her your pulpit to control the congregation with some self-promoting *"the word of the Lord."* If you notice, I said **he** or **she** because the Jezebel spirit can work through anyone. We will see this later in the next chapter that shows that the working of the Jezebel spirit is not limited to women.

The Jezebel Spirit is a Principality
The definition of a principality is a region that is governed or ruled by a prince. We all know that the Lord Jesus is the King of Kings and that the devil is called **"the prince of this world"** and **"the prince of the power of the air"** in John 12:31 and Ephesians 2:2. Therefore, to be effective against her, you have to have a good understanding of the workings of a principality. **A principality seeks influence over nations or those in authority in nations, states, cities, organizations, churches**, etc. It is one of the reasons we are told the following in **Ephesians 6:12**:

> **"For we wrestle not against flesh and blood,** but against **principalities**, against **powers**, against **the rulers of the darkness of this world**, against **spiritual wickedness in high places."**

Never forget that the Jezebel spirit is not a person but a spirit; a demonic spirit in the hand of the devil. **As a result, the devil uses the Jezebel spirit as his powerful tool over whole regions and nations. She operates on the level of a principality and failure to deal with her on this level will result in ineffective warfare against her.** Not only does she have a following in the church today, she has a following (disciples) nationally and internationally. **As a principality, the Jezebel spirit seeks to influence leaders and those that have positions of authority or power in every nation.**

In most cases, if you have no position of authority, the Jezebel spirit does not really get attracted to you because she likes attention and she likes to command other people. She needs to have a realm from which she can command and from which she can send out her false messages and false doctrines. This is why the Lord said that <u>there are those who have her doctrines in them and she has taught them</u> **"the depths of satan" — Revelation 2:24-25.** These people will blatantly challenge you and contend with what is written in the Bible:

> **"But unto you I say, and unto the rest in Thyatira, as many as have not this doctrine, and which <u>have not known the depths of Satan,</u> as they speak;** I will put upon you none other burden. 52 But that which ye have already hold fast till I come."

As God is raising you up, you have to be very careful to discern the Jezebel spirit so that you do not align yourself with her. The key to remember is that a strong and decisive leader who walks in genuine love is usually a threat to her.

She is a Thorn on the Sides of Most Nations

Right now, many nations have active covenants with the Jezebel spirit; especially in the western nations where she has been given liberty to influence moral and social conducts. To go after her means that every one of us Christians has to make sure that this spirit is not operating in us and we do this by "breaking up our fallow ground." The Lord commanded us in **Jeremiah 4:3** to deal with the things in our lives that will make our warfare ineffective; i.e., to break up our fallow ground and not sow among thorns. In this case, it means to remove from our lives those things that the devil and the Jezebel spirit can use to make us fall into her wicked ways:

> "For thus saith the LORD to the men of Judah and Jerusalem, **Break up your fallow ground, and sow not among thorns.**"

When you break up your fallow ground, you can then sow good seeds in the ground without thorns. The result is that you will have a bountiful harvest; in this case, victory over the Jezebel spirit. We have to make sure that we do not have an active covenant with her. I have a book that is titled, ***Understanding the Power of Covenants*** that will help you to learn how to avoid evil covenants. Covenants are very important to God because everything that He does with us is within the context of a covenant.

Chapter 8
The Jezebel Spirit Can Operate Through Men

The Jezebel Spirit is Not Limited by Sex

The Jezebel spirit will work against **any leader** that opens his or her leadership to it. **It works through men and women; it is not limited by sex.** What this means is that any leader who is not effective or is ignorant about the authority that has been vested in him or her, is susceptible to the Jezebel spirit; it can come through a man or a woman. Even strong leaders sometimes exhibit some blind spots in their lives and the Jezebel spirit will take advantage of them in those areas as we are going to see in the case of King David. Remember that some of the Jezebel spirit's tools are lust, sex, manipulation and killing of the innocent.

The Jezebel Spirit and King David

Just as King Herod lusted after Salome; his wife's daughter, King David yielded to the Jezebel spirit through lust. **As the King, he was supposed to be in the battlefield with his soldiers but he decided to stay at home and in his idle time, he began to lust after a married woman as he was watching her take a bath. The Jezebel spirit immediately inspired him to send for her and he did.** In other words, it was because of his sexual lust that King David sent for Bathsheba while knowing fully well that she was married — **2 Samuel 11:1-5:**

> "And it came to pass, after the year was expired, at <u>the time when kings go forth to battle</u>, that David sent Joab, and his servants with him, and all Israel; and they destroyed the children of Ammon, and besieged Rabbah. But David tarried still at Jerusalem. 2 **And it came to pass in an eveningtide, that David arose from off his bed, and walked**

upon the roof of the king's house: and from the roof he saw a woman washing herself; and the woman was very beautiful to look upon *(lust).*

3 And David sent and enquired after the woman. And one said, Is not this Bathsheba, the daughter of Eliam, the wife of Uriah the Hittite? 4 **And David sent messengers, and took her; and she came in unto him, and he lay with her; for she was purified from her uncleanness: and she returned unto her house** *(he abused his power as the King).* 5 **And the woman conceived, and sent and told David, and said, I am with child."**

To cover up his crime of sleeping with another man's wife and getting her pregnant, he devised a plan to manipulate the woman's husband, Uriah in his attempt to hide the fact that the child the woman was carrying was his. He sent for Uriah who was at the battlefield with the rest of the soldiers to be sent to him. When Uriah arrived, King David used his authority to command him to go home to his wife and he gave him a large mesh of meat but Uriah did not go home so King David pretended to be his friend in order to get him drunk. When he successfully got Uriah drunk, he again told Uriah to go home to his wife and Uriah refused.

Actually, King David used his position as the King to command Uriah to go home to his wife but God loved Uriah too much to allow King David to successfully cover up his wickedness by deceiving him. In his response to the King's command to go home to his wife, **Uriah invoked his fear of God and his loyalty to the King and Israel as the reason he would not go home to his wife —2 Samuel 11:6-13:**

"And David sent to Joab, saying, **Send me Uriah the Hittite.** And Joab sent Uriah to David. 7 And when Uriah was come unto him, David demanded of him how Joab did, and how the people did, and how the war prospered. *8* **And David said to Uriah, Go down to thy house, and wash thy feet. And Uriah departed out of the king's house, and there followed him a mess of meat from the king.** *9* <u>**But Uriah slept at the door of the king's house with all the servants of his lord, and went not down to his house.**</u>

And when they had told David, saying, **Uriah went not down unto his house, David said unto Uriah, Camest thou not from thy journey? why then didst thou not go down unto thine house?** *11* **And** <u>**Uriah said unto David, The ark**</u>**,** and <u>**Israel**</u>**,** and <u>**Judah, abide in tents; and my lord Joab, and the servants of my lord, are encamped in the open fields; shall I then go into mine house, to eat and to drink, and to lie with my wife**</u>**?** as thou livest, and as thy soul liveth, I will not do this thing.

12 **And David said to Uriah, Tarry here today also, and tomorrow I will let thee depart.** <u>So Uriah abode in Jerusalem that day, and the morrow.</u> *13* **And when David had called him, he did eat and drink before him; and <u>he made him drunk</u>:** and at even <u>he went out to lie on his bed with the servants of his lord</u>, **but went not down to his house.**"

King David's crime in this matter is <u>one of the most cruel acts</u> that one person can commit against another. **It tells us that the Jezebel spirit can stir up anyone that <u>yields</u> to its <u>sexual lust</u> no matter how strong the person is as leader.** When his manipulating schemes failed to get Uriah to go home and sleep with his wife so that he can pass the unborn child off as Uriah's, he came up with a plan to kill the man and take his wife. **He not** only devised a wicked plan to have Uriah killed but he made Uriah to carry his own execution letter; telling the captain of his army, Joab to make sure that he places Uriah in the part of the battlefield where he would surely be killed — **2 Samuel 11:14-21:**

> "**And it came to pass in the morning, that David wrote a letter to Joab, and <u>sent it by the hand of Uriah</u>.** *15* And <u>he wrote in the letter, saying,</u> **Set ye Uriah in the forefront of the hottest battle, and retire ye from him, that he may be smitten, and die.** *16* And it came to pass, when Joab observed the city, that he assigned Uriah unto a place where he knew that valiant men were.
>
> *17* And the men of the city went out, and fought with Joab: and there fell some of the people of the servants of David; and Uriah the Hittite died also. *18* Then Joab sent and told David all the things concerning the war; *19* And charged the messenger, saying, When thou hast made an end of telling the matters of the war unto the king, *20* And if so be that the king's wrath arise…, **then say thou, Thy servant Uriah the Hittite is dead also.**"

From the above words of Joab, we can see that he was aware of the wickedness that King David plotted against Uriah because of his wife. What King David did to Uriah reminds us of what King Herod's wife, Herodias did to get the head of John the Baptist — manipulation! **Many kings and heads of government have been used by the Jezebel spirit to commit wicked and ungodly acts because of their lustful desires.** For example, many men and women have been known to kill other men and women in order to have their spouses. It all points to the Jezebel spirit and how she uses the tool of lust to inspire people to commit wickedness.

The Jezebel Spirit and Amnon — King David's Son

The Bible tells us that King David was a very powerful King and a mighty warrior. As the King, he had rightly pronounced judgment in just about every case that was brought before him because he knew the Law. **He also knew how God felt about ruling and judging according to the law but when it came to his children, <u>he had a weak spot</u>.** Therefore, when there was an incestuous rape in his household, both as a father and as the King, he did nothing. **This was a serious weakness with consequences that affected not just his household but the entire nation of Israel as we are going to see later.**

In King David's household, the Jezebel spirit stirred up one of his sons named Amnon to lust in a very sick and abominable way after his half-sister, King David's daughter named Tamar. Amnon confided his incestuous lust for his half-sister to his cousin named Jonadab. Just as to be expected, the devil used Jonadab to help Amnon come up with a plan to get his half-sister to his house in order to have his way with her as we see in **2 Samuel 13:1-19:**

> **"And it came to pass after this, that Absalom the son of David had a fair sister, whose name was Tamar; and <u>Amnon the son of David loved her</u>.** 2 **And <u>Amnon was so vexed, that he fell sick for his sister Tamar;</u> for she was a virgin;** and <u>Amnon thought it hard for him to do anything to her</u>. 3 But Amnon had a friend, whose name was <u>Jonadab</u>, the son of Shimeah David's brother: and Jonadab was a very subtil man *(a vessel sent by the devil)*.
>
> 4 And he said unto him, **Why art thou, being the king's son, lean from day to day? wilt thou not tell me?** <u>And Amnon said unto him</u>, **I love Tamar, my brother Absalom's sister.** 5 And <u>Jonadab said unto him</u>, **Lay thee down on thy bed, and make thyself**

sick: and when thy father cometh to see thee, say unto him, I pray thee, let my sister Tamar come, and give me meat, and dress the meat in my sight, that I may see it, and eat it at her hand *(a very wicked counsel from hell).*

6 So Amnon lay down, and made himself sick: and when the king was come to see him, Amnon said unto the king, I pray thee, let Tamar my sister come, and make me a couple of cakes in my sight, that I may eat at her hand *(this should have aroused suspicion in King David).* 7 <u>Then David sent home to Tamar, saying, Go now to thy brother Amnon's house, and dress him meat.</u> 8 So Tamar went to her brother Amnon's house; and he was laid down. And she took flour, and kneaded it, and made cakes in his sight, and did bake the cakes.

9 And she took a pan, and poured them out before him; but he refused to eat. **And Amnon said, Have out all men from me.** And they went out every man from him. 10 And Amnon said unto Tamar, Bring the meat into the chamber, that I may eat of thine hand. And Tamar took the cakes which she had made, and brought them into the chamber to Amnon her brother. 11 **And when she had brought them unto him to eat, he took hold of her, and said unto her, <u>Come lie with me, my sister</u>** *(incest).*

12 **And she answered him, Nay, my brother, do not force me; for no such thing ought to be done in Israel: do not thou this folly.** 13 And I, whither shall I cause my shame to go? and as for thee, thou shalt be as one of the fools in Israel. <u>Now therefore, I pray thee, speak unto the king; for he will not withhold me from thee.</u> 14 **Howbeit he would not hearken unto her voice: <u>but, being stronger than she, forced her, and lay with her.</u>**

15 **Then Amnon hated her exceedingly; so that the hatred wherewith he hated her was greater than the love wherewith he had loved her.** And Amnon said unto her, **Arise, be gone.** 16 And she said unto him, **There is no cause: this evil in sending me away is greater than the other that thou didst unto me. But he would not hearken unto her.** 17 Then he called his servant that ministered unto him, and said, **Put now this woman out from me, and bolt the door after her.**

18 And she had a garment of divers colours upon her: for with such robes were the king's daughters that were virgins apparelled. **Then his servant brought her out, and bolted the door after her.** 19 And Tamar put ashes on her head, and rent her garment of divers colours that was on her, and laid her hand on her head, and went on crying."

As we can clearly see in the account of these events, Amnon's so-called love for Tamar was nothing but lust stirred up in him by the Jezebel spirit. It quickly turned to hatred and he immediately despised her right after he had slept with her. Tamar went home crying and her brother Absalom found out what happened to her. King David also found out what his son Amnon had done to his daughter Tamar and he failed to address it or act according to the Law. **His father's inaction prompted Absalom to take matters into his own hands by avenging his sister's honor —2 Samuel 13:20-39:**

"**And Absalom her brother said unto her, Hath Amnon thy brother been with thee? but hold now thy peace , my sister:** he is thy brother; regard not this thing. So Tamar remained desolate in her brother Absalom's house. 21 **But when king David heard of all these things, he was very wroth.** 22

And Absalom spake unto his brother Amnon neither good nor bad: for Absalom hated Amnon, because he had forced his sister Tamar. 23 **And it came to pass after two full years** *(two years of King David not punishing Amnon according to the Law)*,

that Absalom had sheepshearers in Baalhazor, which is beside Ephraim: and Absalom invited all the king's sons. 24 And Absalom came to the king, and said, Behold now, thy servant hath sheepshearers; let the king, I beseech thee, and his servants go with thy servant. 25 And the king said to Absalom, Nay, my son, let us not all now go, lest we be chargeable unto thee. And he pressed him: howbeit he would not go, but blessed him. 26 <u>Then said Absalom, If not, I pray thee, let my brother Amnon go with us. And the king said unto him, Why should he go with thee?</u>

27 But Absalom pressed him, that he let Amnon and all the king's sons go with him. 28 **Now Absalom had commanded his servants, saying, Mark ye now when Amnon's heart is merry with wine, and when I say unto you, Smite Amnon; then kill him, fear not: have not I commanded you? be courageous, and be valiant.** 29 And the servants of Absalom did unto Amnon as Absalom had commanded...But Absalom fled, and went to Talmai, the son of Ammihud, king of Geshur... 39 **And the soul of king David longed to go forth unto Absalom: <u>for he was comforted concerning Amnon, seeing he was dead.</u>**"

Thus, Absalom avenged his sister's honor by killing his half-brother Amnon; **he did what his father was not willing to do.** Afterwards, Absalom fled to another city. **As to be expected, the Jezebel spirit stirred up King David's**

son, Absalom because it saw the inaction (weakness) that was in King David concerning his children. In other words, according to the Law, King David was supposed to have judged and condemned his son Amnon to death but because he was his son, he ignored the Law. Therefore, Absalom (a Judge in King David's court) took matters into his own hands.

The summary of the matter is that it was the Jezebel spirit that stirred up Amnon to lust after his half-sister. It then stirred up another one of King David's sons (Absalom) to act where his father the King did not act.

The Jezebel Spirit and Absalom

Just as King David did nothing concerning Amnon's sin of raping his half-sister, he also did nothing concerning Absalom's killing of his half-brother, Amnon. As a result, Absalom expected his father to allow him to come back home after years of self-imposed exile so that he can continue in the court as a Judge, but King David did not send for him to return from exile for years. At the persistence of Joab; the Captain of King David's army, the King eventually allowed Absalom to return but not to see his face. King David did not send for Absalom to come to court for over two years until Joab again forced the King's hand and Absalom was allowed to come to court **— 2 Samuel 14: 28-33:**

> **"So Absalom dwelt two full years in Jerusalem, and saw not the king's face...** 32 And Absalom answered Joab, Behold, I sent unto thee, saying, Come hither, that I may send thee to the king, to say, **Wherefore am I come from Geshur? it had been good for me to have been there still: now therefore let me see the king's face; and if there be any iniquity in me, let him kill me.** 33 ...when he *(King David)* had called for Absalom,

he came to the king, and bowed himself on his face to the ground before the king: **and the king kissed Absalom.**"

As you are about to see, the Jezebel spirit can work through a man to usurp the authority of the leader and Absalom is a classic case. Absalom was loved by the people and his resentment towards his father for not allowing him to come to court as a judge for over two years made him begin to "bad mouth" his father and his father's style of judgment. According to **2 Samuel 15:1-6**, he would stand at the gate of his father's palace and tell the people that if he was allowed to judge in the court of the king, he could get them good judgment because the King did not have a good judge like himself. As he did this on a daily basis, Absalom successfully stole the hearts of the people and turned them away from his father the King. **He usurped the God-given authority of his father to rule Israel:**

"And it came to pass after this, that Absalom prepared him chariots and horses, and fifty men to run before him. 2 **And Absalom rose up early, and stood beside the way of the gate: and it was so, that when any man that had a controversy came to the king for judgment, then Absalom called unto him, and said,**

Of what city art thou? And he said, Thy servant is of one of the tribes of Israel. 3 **And Absalom said unto him, See, thy matters are good and right; but there is no man deputed of the king to hear thee.** 4 Absalom said moreover, **Oh that I were made judge in the land, that every man which hath any suit or cause might come unto me, and I would do him justice!**

5 **And it was so, that when any man came nigh to him to do him obeisance, he put forth his hand, and took him, and kissed him.** 6 And on this manner did Absalom to all Israel that came to the king for judgment: **so Absalom stole the hearts of the men of Israel.**"

You can see how Absalom used the Jezebel spirit's tactics of flatteries and usurping of authority to get his way. He not only lobbied for the position of a Judge but he began to desire to unseat the King. In other words, his resentment opened the door for the Jezebel spirit to start nudging him to rise up and overthrow his father as the King. **After some years, he eventually went to Hebron and there proclaimed himself King in place of his father.** He committed a serious act of treason that caused King David to abdicate his throne and to run for his life as recorded in **2 Samuel 15:10-14:**

"**But Absalom sent spies throughout all the tribes of Israel, saying, As soon as ye hear the sound of the trumpet, then ye shall say, Absalom reigneth in Hebron.** 11 And with Absalom went two hundred men out of Jerusalem, that were called; and they went in their simplicity, and they knew not anything. 12 And Absalom sent for Ahithophel the Gilonite, David's counsellor, from his city, even from Giloh, while he offered sacrifices.

And the conspiracy was strong; for the people increased continually with Absalom. 13 And there came a messenger to David, saying, **The hearts of the men of Israel are after Absalom.** 14 And David said unto all his servants that were with him at Jerusalem, Arise, and let us flee; for we shall not else escape from Absalom:** make speed to depart, lest he overtake us suddenly, and bring evil upon us, and smite the city with the edge of the sword."

The Jezebel Spirit and Gehazi — Prophet Elisha's Servant

Besides the fact that the Jezebel spirit operated in leaders such as **Samson, King David** and **King Herod** using lust to make them its slaves to evil desires, it can also operate through assistants to leaders. The man named Gehazi; the Prophet Elisha's servant is a very good example of this. **I included his story because those who are very close or are assistants to God's appointed leaders are very vulnerable to the Jezebel spirit.** Gehazi lost his ministry because of his lust for material things and money.

The Prophet Elisha was so angry with him that he judged him and he became a leper. Gehazi lusted after the money and the gifts that his master rejected from Naaman. **It is a lustful desire that opens up a person to evil spirits for inspiration on how to fulfill the desire.** This is why we are told in **James 1:13-15** that God does not tempt us:

> "Let no man say when he is tempted, I am tempted of God: for God cannot be tempted with evil, neither tempteth he any man: 14 **But every man is tempted, when he is <u>drawn away of his own lust, and enticed.</u>** 15 Then when lust hath conceived, it bringeth forth sin: and sin, when it is finished, bringeth forth death."

The summary of the events is that God used the Prophet Elisha to demonstrate His power to heal by delivering Naaman, the Captain of Syria's army from leprosy. Naaman had come to the Prophet Elisha with great pump and high opinion of himself that the Prophet Elisha cut him down to size by refusing to come out of his house to see or meet him. Instead, he sent a messenger to tell Naaman to go to the River Jordan to bath and be healed. As it is written in **2 King 5:9-14**, he reluctantly went and bathed and was healed:

"So Naaman came with his horses and with his chariot, and stood at the door of the house of Elisha. 10 And Elisha sent a messenger unto him, saying, Go and wash in Jordan seven times, and thy flesh shall come again to thee, and thou shalt be clean. **11 But Naaman was wroth, and went away, and said, Behold, I thought He will surely come out to me, and stand, and call on the name of the LORD his God, and strike his hand over the place, and recover the leper.**

12 <u>Are not Abana and Pharpar, rivers of Damascus, better than all the waters of Israel? may I not wash in them, and be clean? So he turned and went away in a rage</u>... **14 Then went he down, and dipped himself seven times in Jordan, according to the saying of the man of God: and his flesh came again like unto the flesh of a little child, and he was clean.**"

Naaman was impressed and became very grateful for the power of the God of Israel that had healed him of leprosy. To show his gratitude, he wanted the Prophet Elisha to receive the gifts that he brought for him from Syria but Elisha refused Naaman's gifts. He was not willing to receive anything for the healing of Naaman from leprosy because he wanted God to receive all the glory – **2 King 5:15-16:**

"And he *(Naaman)* returned to the man of God, he and all his company, and came, and stood before him: and he said, **Behold, now I know that there is no God in all the earth, but in Israel: <u>now therefore, I pray thee, take a blessing of thy servant.</u> 16 But he *(Elisha)* said, As the LORD liveth, before whom I stand, I will receive none. And he urged him to take it; <u>but he refused.</u>**"

Seeing that his master had rejected Naaman's gifts, Gehazi began to lust after the money and the gifts. **He ran to meet Naaman** and he lied to get the money and the gifts that the Prophet Elisha rejected from Naaman as recorded in **2 Kings 5:20-24:**

> "But Gehazi, the servant of Elisha the man of God, **said, Behold, my master hath spared Naaman this Syrian, in not receiving at his hands that which he brought: but, as the LORD liveth, I will run after him, and take somewhat of him.** 21 So Gehazi followed after Naaman. And when Naaman saw him **running after him**, he lighted down from the chariot to meet him, and said, Is all well? 22 And he said, All is well. **My master hath sent me, saying, Behold, even now there be come to me from mount Ephraim two young men of the sons of the prophets: give them, I pray thee, a talent of silver, and two changes of garments** *(a lie).*
>
> 23 And Naaman said, **Be content, take two talents. And he urged him, and bound two talents of silver in two bags, with two changes of garments, and laid them upon two of his servants; and they bare them before him.** 24 And when he *(Gehazi)* came to the tower, **he took them from their hand, and bestowed them in the house:** and he let the men go, and they departed."

Although the Prophet Elisha was very displeased with what his servant Gehazi had done, he gave him an opportunity to redeem himself or come clean but Gehazi lied to cover his lust for material things. Therefore, the prophet Elisha judged him by sending the leprosy that was upon Naaman on Gehazi – **2 Kings 5:25-27**:

"But he went in, and stood before his master. **And Elisha said unto him, Whence comest thou, Gehazi? And he said, Thy servant went no whither.** 26 And he said unto him, <u>Went not mine heart with thee, when the man turned again from his chariot to meet thee</u>? Is it a time to receive money, and to receive garments, and oliveyards, and vineyards, and sheep, and oxen, and menservants, and maidservants? 27 **The leprosy therefore of Naaman shall cleave unto thee, and unto thy seed forever. And he went out from his presence a leper as white as snow.**"

What Gehazi was not aware of was that the Prophet Elisha had received the Anointing that was upon the Prophet Elijah by faithfully serving the Prophet Elijah. As a result, Gehazi was well positioned to receive the Prophet Elisha's mantle had he too been faithful to the end. We can safely say that the Jezebel spirit cost Gehazi the very important call of God that was upon his life. Also, the Elijah anointing that was upon the Prophet Elisha's life hates the Jezebel spirit. It is an anointing that judges the Jezebel spirit wherever it finds it; it does not fraternize with it.

Chapter 9
The Jezebel Spirit and the Doctrine of Homosexuality

What is Homosexuality?

The dictionary defines homosexuality as "relating to or characterized by a tendency to direct sexual desire toward another of the same sex." It involves sexual intercourse between persons of the same sex. The truth of the matter is that God created **Adam** and **Eve** (not Adam and Steve) as **male** and **female with reproducing organs designed for the continuation of the human race.** This is why it is clearly stated in **Genesis 5:2** that God created Adam and Eve and that He created a <u>male</u> and a <u>female</u>:

"**Male** and **female** created he **them**; and blessed them..."

Not only that, God lets us know in His written Word that homosexuality is a sin before Him; actually, it is <u>an abomination</u> to Him as He declared in **Leviticus 18:22:**

"<u>Thou shalt not lie with mankind, as with womankind</u>: **it is abomination.**"

An abomination is something that is **a grave moral offence;** a cause of abhorrence or disgust. God does not want any human being to practice it hence it was further emphasized in **Romans 1:21-28** that we should stay away from practicing it. God has a horrible judgment awaiting those who disregard His Word about it:

"Because that, when they knew God, they glorified him not as God, neither were thankful; but became vain in their imaginations, and their foolish heart was darkened. 22 Professing themselves to be wise, they became fools...*24* **Wherefore God also gave them up to uncleanness through the <u>lusts of their own hearts</u>, to dishonour their own bodies between themselves:** *25* Who changed the truth of God into a lie, and worshipped and served the creature more than the Creator, who is blessed forever. Amen.

26 **For this cause God gave them up unto <u>vile affections</u>: for even their <u>women did change the natural use into that which is against nature</u>:** *27* **And likewise also <u>the men, leaving the natural use of the woman, burned in their lust one toward another; men with men working that which is unseemly</u>,** and receiving in themselves that recompence of their error which was meet. *28* **And even as they did not like to retain God in their knowledge, God gave them over to <u>a</u> <u>reprobate mind</u>, to do those things which are not convenient..."**

The real name for homosexuality is **sodomy**. The reason is because it was the one or singular sin that the people that lived in a country called Sodom committed that made God to wipe them off the face of the earth. **It made God to regard them as very wicked sinners and because they practiced anal sex or sodomy, it began to be called after them.** In the story of Sodom, we can clearly see how a whole city or nation was given to the practice of sodomy in **Genesis 19:4-25:**

"But before they lay down, **the men of the city, even the men of Sodom, compassed the house round,** <u>both old and young</u>, all the people from every quarter: *5* And they called unto Lot, and said unto him, **Where are the men which came in to thee this night? bring them out unto us, that we may know them** *(in other words, have sex with* *them).* 6 And Lot went out at the door unto them, and shut the door after him, 7 <u>And said, I pray you, brethren, do not so wickedly</u>. 8 Behold now, **I have two daughters which have not known man; let me, I pray you, bring them out unto you, and do ye to them as is good in your eyes: <u>only unto these men do nothing</u>**; for therefore came they under the shadow of my roof.

9 And they said, Stand back. And they said again, **This one fellow came in to sojourn, and he will needs be a judge: now will we deal worse with thee, than with them. And they pressed sore upon the man, even Lot, and came near to break the door**... Then the LORD rained upon Sodom and upon Gomorrah brimstone and fire from the LORD out of heaven; 25 **And he overthrew those cities, and all the plain, and all the inhabitants of the cities, and that which grew upon the ground.**"

These <u>events</u> that took place in Sodom and the <u>corresponding judgment from God</u> shows us that God was not playing when He said that the sin of sodomy is an abomination to Him but the Jezebel spirit seeks to make those who are caught in her web (in her sins) to forget or disregard God's Word about their behavior.

The Doctrine of Homosexuality
The sin of homosexuality is a direct challenge to God (an affront) as the Jezebel spirit that is behind it stirs up those who practice it to blame God for creating them differently from other segments of societies. In other words, the men who are attracted to other men claim to be women that are placed in a man's body while the women claim to be men placed in women's body! **The bottom line is that they all blame God for not knowing the difference between a man and a woman when He was creating them.** Therefore, to

them, God is responsible for their sexual orientation because He created them that way—they are nothing but victims of how God created them!

They echo Lady Gaga's words that, *"I was Born This Way."* This is a lie from the pit of hell because when God finished His creation as it is written in **Genesis 1:31**, God saw that everything that He created **was very good**:

> "**And God saw everything that he had made, and, behold, it was very good.** And the evening and the morning were the sixth day."

From the above scripture, we can clearly see that God in His infinite wisdom knew that a group of people would arise and that they would seek to justify their ungodly behaviors by challenging His creation. Therefore, He made it a point to let us know that everything that He created; including **Adam** and **Eve**, <u>were very good</u>. God cannot lie and as a result, one of His titles is "the God who cannot lie" but the homosexuals call Him a liar everyday by their behavior and their lifestyle. They have totally given the Jezebel spirit permission to use them to accuse God.

Now, the Jezebel spirit is aggressively using the homosexual agenda to try to destroy the moral codes of societies and she encourages those enslaved by her and societies at large to blame their self-indulging perverted lifestyles on God. Because of the wide acceptance of her doctrines in western societies, homosexuals are now fighting for the right to engage in same-sex marriage. They want the same legal rights that a genuine husband and wife enjoy because they have convinced themselves and other segments of society that a man marrying another man and a woman marrying another woman is equal to a man marrying a woman!

Why is the Homosexual Sin Different from Other Sins?

God hates all sins but the homosexual sin is the only sin that begs to be excused and that blames God. **I have always told people that the problem with the sin of homosexuality is that those who practice it do not think that they are doing anything wrong and they actually want to get everyone else to accept them and approve of their lifestyle. <u>They do not want to hear what God's Word says about it.</u>** When it comes to other sins such as lying, stealing, fornication, pornography or adultery, etc., those who commit these sins know within themselves that they are doing something wrong.

For example, when a man or woman commits adultery, there is a certain level of guilt or condemnation because they know that they have done what they were not supposed to do according to God's written and natural law. Otherwise, they will not be seeking to hide their actions or meet in secret places. Also, after their rendezvous, they usually head straight for the shower because none of them want their spouse to smell the fragrance of another person on them or on their clothing. Some people will even place their clothes where their spouse cannot find them. The bottom line is that there is an element of guilt because of God's Word about it and society's moral laws.

In other words, there is a conviction in you that you have done something wrong when you commit any of these sins but the homosexual doctrine is that God made a mistake when He created them. Again, the women say that, "God made me a man but He made a mistake and He lied because He has given me a woman's body." Therefore, they believe that they are doing the right thing by sleeping with other women and the men likewise. **As a result, there is <u>no conviction</u> that their actions constitute a sin before God.**

Those who seek to live by the word of God on the matter are called intolerant and homophobic. For those of us who chose to walk the Christian-walk, we know that God cannot lie and that God does not make mistakes. **The truth of the matter is that none of us would have known what a man or a woman is if God had not told us.** When He started out in the Garden of Eden, He made Adam and Eve <u>to reproduce</u> so that they can populate the earth. **The homosexual doctrine seeks to play this down hence some years ago, Oprah had a TV program with a claim that a "man" was having a baby but the truth of the matter was that the claim was a lie.**

The truth of the story was that the so-called "man" was still a woman because when she went through a sex change operation, she never removed her womb. **Although she was parading herself as a man, she was in all essence still a woman because she still had her womb!** Instead, what the story proved was that she was always a woman. **She thought that just because she had something sown between her legs that she had become a man but the fact that she conceived with her God-given womb proved that God made Adam and Eve and not Adam and Steve!**

God's Definition of a Woman

The God-given definition of a woman is **Adam** (man) **that has a <u>womb</u>; a womb-man** (woman). It is the womb, the ovaries and other female reproductive organs that make the difference. Therefore, when a lady thinks that she has become a man because of some <u>body altering surgery</u> but still retains her womb and other reproductive organs, she is still a woman; she never really became a man. When she marries a man and conceives a baby, it only proves that she was always a woman (a womb-man) because the "truly male" partner who has always been a man cannot do the same. **Also, the definition of a man is a male without a womb and other female reproductive organs.**

<u>These definitions are not complicated, but the Jezebel spirit seeks to change them and to introduce her confusion of</u>

<u>what is a man and a woman in so-called modern societies</u>. To prove the infallibility of this definition above, doctors can get a human egg from a donor and fertilize the egg in a dish (IFV) and place the egg directly into the womb of a woman and she will conceive and give birth but they cannot do that with a man. **Therefore, do not allow the disciples of the Jezebel spirit to twist what you believe according to the Word of God because we are in a very serious time in human history. It is a time in which we have to stand up for what we believe even if it costs us our lives.**

Effects of the Homosexual Doctrine at the Government Level

Currently, the Jezebel spirit's doctrines have great influence on government at every level in a lot of countries and states. As a result, they are fighting for acceptance, recognition, insurance coverage and for everything a husband and wife has God-given rights to and they call it their <u>civil rights</u>. I recently heard someone say that the greatest accomplishment in this decade is the civil rights victory for gays and lesbians! **My thought was when did it become a civil right to practice something that is abominable?** I recently read an article about a man in some country who married his dog. He was going on his honeymoon with his dog spouse!

There was another article about a woman in Britain who also married her dog. As I wondered whether or not bestiality was now legal in some countries, someone told me that it was not illegal in a lot of western countries for people to have sex with their pets! Ask yourself; where does it end? Will that become the next "civil rights" battle? **The truth of the matter is that the homosexual spirit is fiercely intolerant of anyone that tries to tell those who practice it what the Word of God says concerning the lifestyle.** They scream the loudest from every media outlet at their disposal and they think that just because many of them are now working in the news media and in courts as judges, they can shove what God calls an abomination down the throat of Bible believing Christians and society at large.

The fight is increasingly becoming global as some self-appointed nations in western countries are seeking to force the acceptance of homosexuality upon nations who see the abomination that homosexual lifestyle is and legislate against it. They are using the school systems, movies, TV programs and the news media to desensitize the younger generation so that they cannot see the abomination that the homosexual lifestyle represents. The bisexuals are now getting in on the act because they too now want the right to go "both ways" even when they are married.

Married bisexuals are now coming out of the closets because the devil is out to challenge the biblical and moral laws of a lot of countries concerning sexual practices. Also, transgenders are fighting for acceptance and some parents are now dressing up their little children as the opposite sex and demanding the school systems to grant them access to the bathrooms of the opposite sex! Their argument is that if a little boy feels like he is a little girl or a little girl feels like she is a little boy, they should be dressed and treated as such by society. My question to such parents is, if these same little five or six year olds feel like they are a dog, would these parents put them in cage or put a leash on them and walk them around as a dog without a public outcry?

Why are certain parents using their innocent children to pursue the gay agenda? What is funny is that those who pursue the gay agenda ignore the rights of the normal males and females in society at large. I remember an incident that happened to me some years ago. I was in a restaurant and decided to use the restroom but as I was about to push the restroom door open, someone on the inside pushed it before me and we almost ran into each other and a huge male voice came out of this person that was dressed as a "drag queen." It almost freaked me out because I was not expecting a male in a female restroom regardless of how he was dressed. As Christians, it is time to educate our children at home concerning sexuality before they are miseducated outside of the home.

Effects of the Homosexual Doctrine at the Judicial Level

The Jezebel spirit also exercises her influence over the judiciary level of societies. Right now, we are blessed to live in a state where some things are still a "no-no" as in most of the Bible belt states. Because of the influence of the Jezebel spirit, whenever certain states make a law that banishes homosexuality, she stirs up an activist judge to rise up and overturn what has been voted into law by the citizens in that state. Do not be deceived, she has influence in colleges and institutions of higher learning. She uses closet homosexuals to invalidate moral and God-given laws at all levels of society. She is a dangerous spirit.

When you are dealing with her, you are really taking on a whole slew of different things that you did not suspect as you are trying to prevent your beloved child from straying into her homosexual webs. When your child is caught up in her webs, you do truly have your work cut out for you because you have to conduct spiritual warfare at various levels just to free your child from her grips. You have to use God's wisdom to win the battle on your knees.

The Homosexual Doctrine's War With the Church

The homosexual spirit (Jezebel) has influence in some churches and in a lot of community organizations. The new homosexual agenda is to gain legal rights (civil rights) that allows them to come into the Church and twitch around just to rub Christians' faces in their abominable lifestyle without us being able to say anything. To help further their delusion, the Jezebel spirit preaches from the national level, state level, school systems and the mass media that this evil lifestyle is not a sin. I do believe that we are in the time when the Church has to confront this spirit head on in our efforts to live by God's Word.

As a pastor, what would you do when homosexuals come to your church and before the congregation to tell you that they are gay and want to be accepted as such? What would you do when they demand that you conduct their marriage ceremony because it is the law? **As this begins to happen, ministers will have to give up their 501(c)(3) and the corporation status of their churches in order to be able to speak freely without the government coming down on them.** Right now, before you start a ministry, you may need to consider carefully before filing for a 501(c)(3) so that you are not forced by law into the homosexual agenda if it becomes a national law.

I believe that very soon, Christians will stop meeting in churches and begin to meet in home fellowships so that the tax-exempt status of their churches as corporations will not be used to hold them captive to the homosexual agenda. Again, the homosexuals want to be accepted and supported by family members and society at large because after all, that is how God created them. Also, they are to be accepted even in the churches and some churches are already accepting their lifestyle. Some churches even ordain homosexuals as head of their denominations and they have ordained ministers that are homosexuals. **The homosexuals and their supporters do not think that they have to worry about Judgment Day because they believe that they are all going to heaven because it is all about love and God is love.** They all seem to think that Leviticus 8:22 and Romans 1:21-28 do not apply to them.

In the Atlanta metro area, a pastor come out of the closet a few years ago and another homosexual pastor that was his friend said that his being gay does not change anything!

He can carry on his duties and conduct church services as usual because after all, he has been gay all the years that he had been praying for people, laying hands on them and performing marriage ceremonies. His wife or ex-wife came out in support of him as a homosexual pastor and told the congregation that it is not about his lifestyle but about the ministry. According to her, the anointing has not changed so now that the pastor has come out of the closet, it is time to go forward with the ministry.

Another pastor recently came out in support of same-sex marriage rights because according to him, it is all about love. He quoted the Word of God that said to love the Lord thy God and to love your neighbor as yourself. Therefore, to him, if same- sex people are in love, they should be allowed to marry. **When you listen to such ignorant statements, it makes you wonder whose prophet these people have been from the beginning. What type of Bible do they read? Do they really belong to God?** Whose side are they on; God's side or the devil's side? **The answer is that they were never really on God's side.** They are just as the Lord said in **Matthew 12:30:**

> "He that is not with me is against me; and he that gathereth not with me scattereth abroad."

As I stated in one of my books titled: *How to Discern and Expel Evil Spirits,* **the homosexual spirit can be transferred from one person to another.** As a result, I would not sit under someone with this spirit as my spiritual head or covering; neither will I allow him or her to lay hands on me for any ceremony. If you are spiritually discerning and you allow someone with a contrary spirit to lay their hands on you, you will begin to see all kinds of dysfunctional spirits that you did not bargain for trying to come into your life. Therefore, be very careful of who you allow to lay hands on you and do not listen to the Jezebel doctrines. Always remember that if you make contact with someone carrying a contrary spirit and the spirit begins to express itself against you, you can always bring that contract under the blood of Jesus and renounce the contact before rebuking the spirit in the name of the Lord Jesus. Therefore, never be afraid that someone can permanently give you a spirit that you have not agreed to.

A Biblical Description of the Workings of the Jezebel Spirit

The following is also how the Bible describes the Jezebel spirit and her tactics in **Proverbs 7:1-27:**

"My son, keep my words, and lay up my commandments with thee. 2 Keep my commandments, and live; and my law as the apple of thine eye. 3 Bind them upon thy fingers, write them upon the table of thine heart. 4 Say unto wisdom, Thou art my sister; and call understanding thy kinswoman: 5 **That they may keep thee from the strange woman, from the stranger which flattereth with her words.**

6 <u>For at the window of my house I looked through my casement,</u> 7 **And beheld among the simple ones, I discerned among the youths, a young man void of understanding, 8 Passing through the street near her corner; and he went the way to her house,** 9 In the twilight, in the evening, in the black and dark night: 10 **And, behold, there met him a woman with the attire of an harlot, and subtil of heart.**

11 (She is loud and stubborn; her feet abide not in her house: 12 **Now is she without, now in the streets, and lieth in wait at every corner.)** 13 **So she caught him, and kissed him, and with an impudent face said unto him,** 14 <u>I have peace offerings with me; this day have I payed my vows.</u> 15 **Therefore came I forth to meet thee, diligently to seek thy face, and I have found thee.**

16 **I have decked my bed with coverings of tapestry, with carved works, with fine linen of Egypt.** *17* I have perfumed my bed with myrrh, aloes, and cinnamon. *18* **Come, let us take our fill of love until the morning: let us solace ourselves with loves.** *19* **For the goodman is not at home, he is gone a long journey:** *20* He hath taken a bag of money with him, and will come home at the day appointed.

21 **With her much fair speech she caused him to yield, with the flattering of her lips she forced him.** *22* **He goeth after her straightway, as an ox goeth to the slaughter, or as a fool to the correction of the stocks;** *23* **Till a dart strike through his liver; as a bird hasteth to the snare, and knoweth not that it is for his life.**

24 Hearken unto me now therefore, O ye children, and attend to the words of my mouth. *25* Let not thine heart decline to her ways, go not astray in her paths. *26* **For she hath cast down many wounded: yea, many strong men have been slain by her.** *27* <u>**Her house is the way to hell, going down to the chambers of death.**</u>"

And also **Proverbs 5:1-11**:

"My son, attend unto my wisdom, and bow thine ear to my understanding: *2* That thou mayest regard discretion, and that thy lips may keep knowledge. *3* For the lips of a strange woman drop as an honeycomb, and her mouth is smoother than oil: *4* But her end is bitter as wormwood, sharp as a twoedged sword. *5* **Her feet go down to death; her steps take hold on hell.** *6* Lest thou shouldest ponder the path of life, her ways are moveable, that thou canst not know them... *8* **Remove thy way far**

from her, and come not nigh the door of her house:
9 Lest thou give thine honour unto others, and thy years unto the cruel: 10 Lest strangers be filled with thy wealth; and thy labours be in the house of a stranger; 11 And thou mourn at the last, when thy flesh and thy body are consumed."

The above biblical description confirms the vision of the Jezebel spirit that I am about to narrate below. Her house is truly the way to hell and her belly contains the chambers of death.

My Visions of the Jezebel Spirit

Some years ago, the Lord showed me a vision of the Jezebel spirit in a sprawl and I was shocked at what I saw.

Vision #1:

In this vision, the Jezebel spirit was a very huge woman. She was totally naked and she laid on her back with both her legs spread wide open on I-285 in Atlanta. It is one of the most jarring visions that I have ever seen. I mean, her legs were so wide open in broad daylight that she left nothing for a person's imagination as she bared it all! As I watched in this vision, I noticed that lots of people were <u>driving their cars</u> into her belly through her private parts. Some other people were going into her <u>riding their bicycles</u>, while some were <u>running</u>, <u>jogging</u> or <u>walking</u> into her.

*I even saw a guy whose car had broken down trying to <u>tow his car</u> into her! Her private parts were nothing but a major highway. I was shocked at how so many people were doing everything within their power to get into her and while still in the vision, **I began to wonder why the people were so determined to get into her.** It was then that the Lord showed me the inside of her belly. When I looked into the inner part of her belly,*

I saw that there were chambers inside of her belly that were like different rooms.

In these chambers were men in different sexual acts with other men, women in sexual acts with other women, men and women in sexual acts with animals, and there was a major room in which a mass orgy of different sexual acts were going on. I even saw a room in which men and women clad in leather outfits and dog chains were chained to the walls while the ones that were unchained held whips with which they treated the chained ones like slaves. I saw all kinds of sexual perversions and wickedness taking place inside her belly. As I watched her on I-285, I realized that she was a very broad way that leads people to hell and her major weapons are sex and sexual perversions.

This vision confirmed what the Bibles says about the broad way that leads to destruction. Her belly is truly a road to destruction. She lies flat on her back in the cities of this country and other countries and her legs are wide open for anybody walking, riding a bicycle or driving car to have access into her; however you can get in, she wants you to come. **This is the reason why many young people are being easily sold on her ways because her ways appeal to the flesh and having an <u>amoral</u> society** (society without morals) **allows her to traffic in sex and other vices.** It took me a long time to get the images of her and what goes on in her belly out of my head because she was out there just letting it hang out.

If you have ever wondered what the Jezebel spirit is really like, then, the vision above shows us her true nature and her web of snares; it is all tied to her private parts. Having seen this vision of the Jezebel spirit, I am amazed when I go to some places and I see a casino advertisement depicting a woman with her legs up in the air. Those who put up the ads know that trafficking in sex and sexual perversions pays off big time but what they do not know is that they are children of the Jezebel spirit. This is why we need to revisit what the Lord said about her in **Revelation 2:18-23:**

> "Notwithstanding I have a few things against thee, **because thou sufferest that woman Jezebel**, which calleth herself a prophetess, to teach **and to seduce my servants to commit fornication,** and to eat things sacrificed unto idols. 21 **And I gave her space to repent of her fornication; and she repented not.** 22 Behold, I will cast her into a bed, and them that commit adultery with her into great tribulation, except they repent of their deeds. 23 **And I will kill her children with death;** and all the churches shall know that I am he which searcheth the reins and hearts..."

The Lord knows that the Jezebel spirit uses her children to promote her agenda and He promised to kill them along with her. Therefore, if you have been living your life as one of her children, my advice to you is to repent and flee from fornication and from her ways.

Vision #2

Some months ago, the Lord again showed me a vision of the Jezebel spirit but this time, the devil was carrying her himself. He was on a rampage as he carried her and was jumping from one house roof-top to another.

As I wondered what it meant, the Lord made me to understand that the devil was taking her to different homes in his attempt to spread sexual perversions in people's bedrooms! As a result, I say that you must be careful not to allow this spirit into your bedroom; even if you are already married because, according to **Hebrews 13:4**, God does not want us to defile our marital beds.

"**Marriage is honourable in all, and the bed undefiled**: but whoremongers and adulterers God will judge."

We must keep our bodies and the marriage bed holy and pure because the devil can still try to pervert it even if you are already married. This is why some Christians need to abide by God's standard concerning acts like oral sex, anal sex, pornography and other people in the marital bed. True Christians should keep themselves from these things as specified in **2 Corinthians 6:17-18:**

"Wherefore **come out from among them, and be ye separate**, saith the Lord, and **touch not the unclean thing; and I will receive you,** 18 And will be a Father unto you, and ye shall be my sons and daughters, saith the Lord Almighty."

God's Criteria for Having a Successful Ministry in this Country

One of the things that the Lord said to me about starting a ministry in this country was: "You have to overcome *(defeat)* the spirit of homosexuality and the spirit of gluttony in order to have a successful ministry in this country." **While the spirit of gluttony seeks to weight people down so that they cannot easily move about to accomplish anything in their lives for God, the homosexual spirit seeks to pervert and change God's established order of relationship in the family between a man and a woman. It wants to defeat God's agenda for the family and for society at large.**

She further seeks to make people debase themselves by engaging in relationships that will lead them to eternal damnation in hell. This is why the Jezebel spirit seeks to create an amoral society; she loves a society where there are no moral laws to restrict her activities. The devil and his agents know that they are going down to hell and they want to take as many human beings with then as they can.

Chapter 10
How to Discern the Jezebel Spirit

She Is Attracted to the Head or the Leader

Today, we see various ungodly activities packaged in ways that make it difficult to identify the Jezebel spirit as the force behind them. When someone tells you that they are up against the Jezebel spirit, you must first recognize as I said earlier that you are dealing with a principality. Meaning that the spirit targets the heads of nations, state, cities, business, homes and other gatherings. She is attracted to whoever is the head or the leader; man or woman.

This is why the battle starts in the home after the man (the head of the home) and the woman say, "I do." She seek to strip the man off all his dignity and she will devalue him to the point that he feels worthless. She can also use sex to control and manipulate him to do what she wants as she tries to assert herself as the boss. It is interesting that in this country, a lot of men have basically accepted their wives as the boss in their homes and they joke about it! **To illustrate this point, the Lord gave me a vision once about a man and his new bride in this country. He wanted me to see how the Jezebel spirit launches into action as soon as the wedding ceremony is over.** Here it is:

> *In this vision, I saw a bridegroom and the bride getting into their bedroom right after the wedding. Both of them were still in their wedding outfits and as soon as they got into the bedroom, the bride immediately picked up the bridegroom and placed him on her kneels like a little baby! I was wondering what this meant when the Lord said to me, that in this society, a lot of the women treat their husbands like their children. He said that spiritually, the minute the man allows his wife to refer to him as "baby," he immediately relinquishes his position as the head of the home and takes on a subservient position in which the wife tells him what to do!*

This is one of the reasons why the cry of most men in our society today is that they are not allowed to be the head in the home. Also, if the man is not pulling his weight financially in the home, the Jezebel spirit will stir up the wife to boss him around and treat him like one of her children because she provides the finances for the home. Therefore, always remember that the Jezebel spirit looks for a vacuum; be it a financial or leadership vacuum, and she will move in to fill it. Most of the people under her influence will not agree that they have done something wrong. Some of them will even use scriptures to justify why they have turned their spouses into one of their children.

She Uses Sex to Promote Her Ways

Prostitution is a national problem and gambling is a national problem. Whole cities are devoted to promoting her sexual ways; cities like Las Vegas and Atlantic City to name a few. Those who traffic in sexual perversions and gambling also target Indian reservations in their attempts to spread sex and gambling to innocent people. As a result of their promotion of sexual perversions, when you look at many of the TV programs today, you will see that advertisers want to sell you things with half-naked women. When you try to watch a movie, it is all about sex; they show you how people meet in the movies and after they say hi, the next thing you know, they are tearing at each other in sexual scenes. The result is that innocent young boys who watch these movies are being trained to expect sex from a girl when they go out on a first date.

The TV programs and movies are preaching the Jezebel spirit's doctrine that right after you meet someone, it is OK to have sex as a way of getting to know them. One of the problems is that these boys and girls are not equipped to handle the responsibilities that come from having protected and unprotected sex but the media is educating them otherwise. The major media outlets have found out that one of the ways that they can flourish is using the tools of the Jezebel spirit. Sex in this country has done more damage to people, to relationships and to marriages than any other thing.

Sex outside of marriage is one of the major killers of marriage in our society and when you look at those who the married people fool around with, they do not even hold a candle to their spouses. So, why do they fool around? The Jezebel spirit found their weakness in the area of sex and she exploits it. **At the end, she pulls the spouses apart, scatters the whole family unit and leaves the children disenfranchised and resentful.** She loves to produce a generation that will suffer and make their own children suffer as they become rebellious and resentful because of their parents' divorce. Many of them join gangs, use drugs and get in and out of prison.

She Uses Addiction to Enslave Her Victims
The Jezebel spirit uses sexual addiction to enslave people to pornography as well as pervert sexual practices and desires. Those who are caught in her sexual webs find it very difficult to get free of the ungodly lifestyle and desires that she drives them into. As a result, our society is full of people who are addicted to sexual sins, drugs and who get into all kinds of trouble. These people struggle to kick the evil lifestyle that they have become addicted to since being ensnared by her.

Pornographic websites, private and public masturbation, uncontrollable visits to strip clubs, visits to prostitutes and rape are some of things that these people struggle with. Even within the context of the marriage covenant, some people cannot seem to get free of these evil habits. If you have been struggling with these sexual vices, know that you are dealing with the Jezebel spirit and that you have to deal with the covenants that you or the generations before you made with her before you can be set free from her web.

She Uses Any Means Possible to Get Her Way

Besides sex, seduction and manipulation, the Jezebel spirit can use <u>vicious and violent means</u> to get her way when someone opposes her. **Although she hates to submit to authority, she will not tolerate anyone who does not submit to her or who refuses to do her will.** She will humiliate those who had previously obeyed her but now oppose her. This is one of the reasons that you see some of the people who are not yet totally free of her ways fall into the very sins that they had publicly spoken against or that they had been fighting to eradicate; she makes a public spectacle of them.

For example, you may have read news articles on several occasions about ministers or people who set out to fight against the homosexual lifestyle and how they became trapped into the lifestyle themselves and were shamed publicly. One of the main reasons is because they were not prepared to go up against her; especially if they or the generations before them were previously into the lifestyle. **You cannot be bound up in any sexual sin when you rise up against her because she will immediately seek out your weakness and without the protection of the Lord, she will try to ensnare you into her web of sexual sins.**

She is authoritarian, bossy and she is angered by those who question or try to hold her accountable. **She is domineering and wants nothing but absolute submission.** Her strongest weapons are sex, addiction, control and manipulation; she is the ultimate manipulator of those who fall for her charms and her flatteries. She has used sex to ruin even world leaders and heads of governments. She uses sex to control men in the bedroom through their wives.

She is Unforgiving

The Jezebel spirit is unforgiving. This spirit can target a person and work on destroying the person for years because of an actual or perceived wrong. Remember the popular saying that, "Hell has no fury like a woman scorned?" This saying typifies the rage and the unforgiving nature of the Jezebel spirit. You saw her reaction through King Ahab's wife when the Prophet Elijah killed the prophets of Baal and also through Herodias when John the Baptist tried to hold her and her husband King Herod morally accountable.

In our daily lives, we have to make sure that our unforgiveness does not open us up to the Jezebel spirit to inspire us on how to get revenge and retaliation. Our Christian faith is based on forgiveness so, forgiveness should come easily for us because we know that God so loved us that He gave His only begotten Son to die for us. He did it while we were still bound up in sin — **Romans 5:7-8:**

> "For scarcely for a righteous man will one die: yet peradventure for a good man some would even dare to die. *8* **But God commendeth his love toward us, in that, <u>while we were yet sinners</u>, Christ died for us.**"

Because God showed us mercy and extended His forgiveness to us, He rises up against those who refuse to forgive others when they are done wrong. The Lord Jesus told us this in **Matthew 18:34-35:**

> "And his lord was wroth, and **delivered him to the tormentors,** till he should pay all that was due unto him. *35* **So likewise shall my heavenly Father do also unto you, if ye from your hearts forgive not everyone his brother their trespasses.**"

She is Behind the Unmarried Lifestyle

The Jezebel spirit does not only raise up false prophets, she also raises unmarried maidens to serve her. <u>She hates the covenant of marriage and will do anything in</u>

or outside of marriage to sabotage any marriage. This is where the unmarried part of the definition of Jezebel comes from. **One of the reasons is because Baal worshippers had unmarried women called "Temple Women." Part of the worship of Baal involved sexual orgy, so they had women in the temple whose job it was to provide "sexual cleansing" services for those that wanted to offer Baal sexual worship.** These women freely slept around and conducted all kinds of debauchery acts within the temple in the worship of their god, Baal.

Outside of Israel, there were also the "Vestal Virgins" that were equally unmarried just like other idol worship practices around the world that require their priestesses to be unmarried. The Bible tells us that it is against God's Word to tell another person not to marry as a requirement for serving God. Yet, we have a certain denominations with this requirement and as a result, there are a lot of sexual misconducts by their priests. **When you place this ungodly demand on people, you open the door for the Jezebel spirit to draw them into the homosexual lifestyle or other sexual sins.**

This is one of the reasons why when you read the news, you normally see that many of them have fallen into the worst types of sexual sins. An unmarried requirement makes the priests vulnerable to the Jezebel spirit who knows how to set them up as her own personal priests or maidens to wallow in sexual sins. **Also, you must recognize her as the ultimate Madam that works in pimps, some casinos owners and some brothel owners. She is even behind the so-called exclusive and high class Escort Services Providers that use men and women as prostitutes.**

She Hates the Institution of Marriage

I recently read that now, less than half of the population in this nation are in a sanctified married relationship and

I did not have to wonder why because all I had to do was look at how the Jezebel spirit goes after the institution of marriage to pull it down and to make it become irrelevant. In other words, she is trying to make marriage become unnecessary in our society so that everyone can live in sin and at the end, incur the wrath of God. You can her agents preaching that, *"You do not have to get married if you and your partner are happy."*

There are some people who think that because they and their partners have been living together for years without being married, that they are blessed and that their relationships are equal to those who are married. Also, you can hear her prophets in the media and other parts of society advocating for people to just live together and have babies without the covenant of marriage because after all, a lot of people are getting divorced! With the help of Hollywood, they make living in sin look cool.

What people have to remember is that marriage is the first institution that God setup as soon He created Adam and Eve; it was before anything in human society and government. The institution of marriage was before the fall of man, before our salvation and before the need to minister or get a job; it was before anything else in human affairs. As a result, God loves the family unit and He blesses it as it is written in **Proverbs 18:22:**

> **"Whoso findeth a wife findeth a good thing,** and obtaineth favour of the LORD."

Most people are not aware that the day a man marries a woman, he receives a blessing from the Lord and he is protected by God. However, when he leaves his wife or takes a mistress, he steps away from God's protection and opens the door for the Jezebel spirit to come into his life and into his home. This is why we read in the news media all the time about how a mistress airs recorded conversations and the dirty laundry of her lover to his shame and disgrace. It is the work of the Jezebel spirit designed to bring the man to shame because he stepped out of God's protection over his marriage.

Today, young people are seeing endless role models of the Jezebel spirit parading their ungodly "outside of marriage" and "modern families" lifestyle before them. Being faithful or avoiding fornication does not come to play in their relationship because it is none existent with them. This is one of the reasons why Hollywood does great destruction to the institution of marriage. God's people are preaching the Word of God from the pulpit but what Hollywood shows the teens that are in the movie theater on Friday and Saturday nights is the direct opposite of the Word of God that they heard growing up.

It makes it hard on the parents because when the children come home and the parents try to talk to them, all they hear from their children is that they (the parents) "do not understand" because to the children, everybody is doing it. They see it on TV and they watch it at the movies. This is how the Jezebel spirit is undermining marriage and parenting in our society today. **Also, try talking to your child that is caught up in the homosexual lifestyle and he or she will tell you that they were created that way. What is worst is that they can pull studies that are contrary to the Word of God but backed by the ungodly agents of the Jezebel spirit to justify their claim.**

Now, parents have to fight hard to keep the claws of the Jezebel spirit away from their children. As Christians, we know that we already have the victory in Christ Jesus and that we can remove this spirit from our home and from our children by believing and speaking the Word of God. Therefore, we must speak the Word of God in faith.

She is Covetous, Lustful and She Entraps

The Jezebel spirit covets power, positions, souls, people's spouses, etc. She is also the spirit of lusts. She uses covetousness and lust as tools to achieve her desired goals. **You can usually discern her agents as they prance and parade their body parts publicly in order to incite lust.** The spirit is shameless as she tries to entrap her victims in order to destroy them.

After she has made them to compromise their positions of authority, she then proceeds to shame them. You can read or listen to the news about how she brings great men to shame and how she disgraces them nationally and internationally with illicit activities, fornication, adultery, perversions and other sexual sins. This is why God said the following in **Proverbs 6:32-33:**

"But whoso committeth adultery with a woman lacketh understanding: he that doeth it destroyeth his own soul. 33 **A wound and dishonour shall he get; and his reproach shall not be wiped away.**"

Everyone will do well to always remember that one of her tools is sex and she will use it to bring anyone that fraternizes with her to nothing. She will make a public spectacle of the person and destroy the person's reputation. Remember one former President? He left the presidency with a balanced budget but today, when you mention his name, people immediately remember the reproach of the infidelity that came upon him and he cannot erase it. It obscured his presidential accomplishments.

I remember a lady in one of the companies where I used to work. She was a heavy set lady but rather than wear dresses that gave her some dignity, she always managed to squeeze herself into some very tight skirts or mini dresses. As a result, she always looked vulgar and outright nasty. On many occasions, I watched as people stopped and made comments about her in unflattering ways. One day, I was alone with her in the ladies' room and she knew that I was a minister so I decided to address her style of dressing. When I told her that every time I saw her, she was always fighting with her clothes, she told me that it was her way of dressing that gives her raises in her paycheck.

In other words, she knew exactly what she was doing; she was purposely dressing that way in order to use lust to keep the attention of her manager. What she did not know was that she had yielded herself to the Jezebel spirit as a tool to promote lust and to entrap her manager. Many men and women have lusted after other people's spouses to the point that they successfully convinced their victims to abandon their spouses and children and begin an ungodly relationship with them.

The Bible warned us to flee from fornication because the Jezebel spirit uses sexual temptation to draw even very powerful people to compromise their ways so that she can bring them down or destroy them. God's impending judgment of the Jezebel spirit is outline in **Revelation 18:4-13:**

> "And I heard another voice from heaven, saying, **Come out of her, my people, that ye be not partakers of her sins, and that ye receive not of her plagues.** 5 **For her sins have reached unto heaven, and God hath remembered her iniquities.** 6 Reward her even as she rewarded you, and double unto her double according to her works: in the cup which she hath filled fill to her double. 7 How much she hath glorified herself, and lived deliciously, so much torment and sorrow give her: for she saith in her heart, I sit a queen, and am no widow, and shall see no sorrow.

8 Therefore shall her plagues come in one day, death, and mourning, and famine; and she shall be utterly burned with fire: for strong is the Lord God who judgeth her. 9 **And the kings of the earth, who have committed fornication and lived deliciously with her, shall bewail her, and lament for her, when they shall see the smoke of her burning,** 10 Standing afar off for the fear of her torment, saying, Alas, alas, that great city Babylon, that mighty city! for in one hour is thy judgment come. 11 And the merchants of the earth shall weep and mourn over her; for no man buyeth their merchandise any more:

12 The merchandise of gold, and silver, and precious stones, and of pearls, and fine linen, and purple, and silk, and scarlet, and all thyine wood, and all manner vessels of ivory, and all manner vessels of most precious wood, and of brass, and iron, and marble, 13 And cinnamon, and odours, and ointments, and frankincense, and wine, and oil, and fine flour, and wheat, and beasts, and sheep, and horses, and chariots, and **slaves,** and **souls of men.**"

She is the Queen of Heaven

The Jezebel spirit exercises her religious influence and control under many titles and being the **Queen of Heaven** is just one of them. <u>You will see her in many pagan religions where the woman is the head and is worshipped</u>. **Therefore, when you are dealing with the queen of heaven in the spiritual realm, you are dealing in the realm of the Jezebel spirit because what she likes is power over nations and over the people who are in authority.** She loves preeminence and attention because she goes back to the time of Nimrod; the first ruler of organized society (the world). **She operated through**

Nimrod's wife and together, they taught the human race idolatry. She presided over religious affairs under the rule of Nimrod.

While Nimrod was known as the **Sun-god**, his wife became known as the **Queen of Heaven and their son Tammuz** as the child-god or the "seed of the woman." They originated **"the unholy trinity"** because Nimrod's wife saw herself as the woman that God spoke of in the Garden of Eden and her son as the "seed of the woman" that would bruise the head of the serpent. I wrote about this in one of my books titled, *Unveiling the God-mother, pages 69-79*. This spirit is out to get control over nations because she has not forgotten that she once ruled the whole world through Nimrod and his wife. Always remember that as the Queen of heaven, her desire is to reign over nations and to change their God-given moral codes because she hates a morally upright society. Therefore, she is against all that are holy and she is against God.

She is at the Head of Witches Covens

One of the major tools in the activities of the Jezebel spirit is the practice of witchcraft. She controlled King Ahab through divination and witchcraft. As a result, a lot of the people that are under the influence of the Jezebel spirit are easily drawn or attracted to organizations that are headed by agents of the spirit. This is why those who practice witchcraft or who are into witchcraft activities can easily pledge their support, membership and loyalty to the high priestess in a witches' coven. They will rally around their so-called high priestess as they pursue the devil's agenda for them. Even in the African type of witchcraft, the witches usually confess that for their nightly meetings, they fly as birds to meet with their queen somewhere in the spiritual realm.

Those who join witches' covens know exactly what they are signing up for and they are well aware of the goals of their individual and general covens. They become the agents that the Jezebel spirit uses to carry out her witchcraft activities.

In the deception that they have received some type of super-natural power, some even boast of their evil connections with the queen of heaven but what they are not aware of is that they have sold their souls to the devil. **But as Born Again Christians, we know that they have no power over us because when we invoke the name of Jesus, every knee bows according to the Word of God in Philippians 2:9-11:**

"Wherefore God also hath highly exalted him, and given him a name which is above every name: 10 **That at the name of Jesus every knee should bow, of things in heaven, and things in earth, and things under the earth;** 11 And that every tongue should confess that Jesus Christ is Lord, to the glory of God the Father."

She Desires a Prominent Platform

The goal of the Jezebel spirit is to kill all of God's people; especially the leaders for their God-given platforms. She perceives them to be in her way and against her agenda. As a result, she wants to make sure that all righteous voices of God's leaders are silenced, removed or made ineffective in societies. This is why, when someone comes to you and says, *"I am dealing with the Jezebel spirit,"* you need to find out what the person is really dealing with. The reason is because in most cases, the Jezebel spirit is only interested in things that give her power, control or the limelight.

She needs a platform from which to operate and it is the reason that she targets people that have authority or influence that can give her the platform from which to influence or pervert a nation or a city. Because the Jezebel spirit seeks to spread her spiritual wickedness, she is not content to operate where there is no authority or influence.

Summary of the Ways to Identify the Jezebel Spirit
- She teaches idolatry and false doctrines
- She uses witchcraft

- She usurps authority because she enjoys the position of power
- She is anti-Christ
- She manipulates
- She is unforgiving, loves revenge and retaliation
- She likes to control people, places and things
- She is very confrontational
- She intimidates (her message to Elijah scared Elijah)
- She uses seduction and sex as entrapment tools
- She promotes whoredom
- She promotes unmarriedness
- She seeks the destruction of leaders
- Her Goal is to kill God's people

Chapter 11
How to Expel the Jezebel Spirit

Power Over Nations
Before going after the Jezebel spirit, you have be armed with the following knowledge; God gives you power over nations when you defeat her! **One of the reasons is because the Jezebel spirit's main desire is to rule nations. Therefore, overcoming her means freeing nations and occupying where she had been exercising her dominion.** <u>This is why the Lord Jesus promised to reward those who overcome the Jezebel spirit with power over nations</u> in **Revelation 2:24-28.** This means being given a spiritual sphere of influence from the Lord and authority to reign over principalities, nations, states and cities:

"But unto you I say, and unto the rest in Thyatira *(those who have not committed adultery with Jezebel)*, as many as have not this doctrine, and which have not known **the depths of Satan,** as they speak; I will put upon you none other burden *(requirement).* 25 But that which ye have already hold fast till I come. 26 **And he that overcometh, and keepeth** **my works unto the end, to him will I give power** **over the nations:** 27 **And he shall rule them with a rod of iron; as the vessels of a potter shall they be broken to shivers: even as I received of my Father.** 28 And I will give him the morning star."

Jezebel is one of the most wicked spirits and we see the Lord calling her "the depths of satan" in the scripture above. As a result, when you go after the Jezebel spirit, you are asking the Lord to give you power over nations because you seek to end her reign over nations. From the above reward promised by the Lord, we can see the extent of the power of the Jezebel spirit when it comes to nations. **The following are keys to overcoming and expelling the Jezebel spirit.**

Recognize the Anointing Upon Your Life

Recognize the anointing upon your life and place a great value on it. The reason God placed Samson's story in the Bible is to teach us not to play around with the anointing upon our lives. Samson had a great calling upon his life but he lacked discipline when it came to women and the devil used that one weakness to prematurely remove him from the earth realm after humiliating and debasing him. The worst thing that can happen to a person is to be delivered into the hands of the person's enemies.

That was exactly what happened to Samson and the Philistines mock him on a daily basis. They made him into their donkey to grind at the mill for them while they laughed and mocked him. None of us can fully imagine how a very powerful warrior like Samson was brought down to a laughing stock by his enemies; it is a very sad story but God meant for us to learn from it. Therefore, be careful of your desires and your actions. **Make it a priority to place a great value on the Anointing of God upon your life so that you do not give room to the Jezebel spirit to have a stronghold in your life.** What I am saying is, do not be reckless with the gifts that God has given you.

Recognize When a Person or a Spirit is After Your Life

We must recognize our enemies. Just because we are to love everyone does not mean that we are to be blind about those who hate us and intend to harm us. The Bible says, "Love your enemies" but it never said to make your enemies your friends. In other words, avoid people that will lead you to destruction. Do not make friends with those that I call, "unfriendly friends." The Bible says the following in **Amos 3:3:**

"Can two walk together, except they be agreed?"

What this tells us is that we are to walk with like-minded people every day of our lives. It does not mean that we are not to have any dealings with unbelievers but we must be careful to know who is really on God's side before we can make them a part of our daily lives. **Also, as God's chosen vessel, you must recognize when a person or a spirit is <u>sent against</u> you by human or spiritual forces and purpose not to fraternize with the person or the spirit.** Failure to do this might lead to your downfall or destruction. What a lot of people are not aware of is that satan sends his agents (spirits or people under his influence) to <u>hunt for and to trade</u> **human souls — Revelation 18:11-13:**

> "And the <u>merchants of the earth</u> shall weep and mourn over her, for no man buyeth their <u>merchandise</u> any more: 12 <u>The merchandise</u> of gold, and silver, and precious stones, and of pearls, and fine linen, and purple, and silk, and scarlet, and all thyine wood, and all manner vessels of ivory, and all manner vessels of most precious wood, and of brass, and iron, and marble, 13 And cinnamon, and odours, and ointments, and frankincense, and wine, and oil, and fine flour, and wheat, and beasts, and sheep, and horses, and chariots, **and slaves, and souls of men.**"

These types of people can be serious spiritual assignments or "Judas" against you. For example, a teenager <u>who is not yet saved</u> might say that he or she does not use drugs and it might be true but running around with "friends" who do, may one day place him or her in a bad place that allows the devil to steal his or her soul through a fatal event. This is one of the reasons why you hear in the news that some teenager went out with a friend and the friend was drunk or reckless with the car and caused an accident that killed them both. Sometimes, the friend survives and the one who had no business being in the car gets killed.

Other times, there can be a shootout and the teenager becomes one of the victims. When this happens, the "friend" has successfully delivered the teenager's soul to the devil. If not for the teenager's "friend," the devil would not have had access to the teenager. This is not limited to teenagers because we read of all types of people being killed by either gunshots, drugs or accidents. Some just get lured into sinful acts or sinful ways by their "friend" or "friends."

Avoid False Doctrines

Do not give room to doctrines that are not biblical. In other words, avoid extra biblical teachings. Many people have been led astray by false doctrines so, do not be one of them. Live by what the Bible says no matter what others are teaching or practicing. This is very critical right now because of what people are promoting that are clearly not acceptable to God. **Most people in western societies are choosing to ignore God's Word concerning moral behavior because they think that He is democratic and that He seeks to extend rights to people to practice whatsoever they believe and to live any way that they please. The truth of the matter is that God is operating a Kingdom where only His Word matters.** A lot of people will find this to be the painful truth on Judgment Day when they come face-to-face with Him.

Those who ignore this day with their Maker will leave Him no choice but to send them to hell to join the devil whose ways they chose. Right now, they are throwing in their lot with him lock, stock and barrel. As a result, they have the loudest voices in society as they try hard to convince people that what they are doing is right and should be accepted. We who are Christians need to remember that the Jezebel spirit has her own prophets in societies that use the platforms of governments, legislators, judges, school systems, media, etc., to shout her doctrines. You will do well to stay away from them because they are the children of the Jezebel spirit. Staying away from them will shut the door against the Jezebel spirit in your life.

Renounce All Past Witchcraft and Occult Activities

You have to renounce all past witchcraft and occult activities in your family and in your life if you want to be free of the Jezebel spirit. Sometimes, these activities were practiced by the generations before you but the fact that the people are now dead does not preclude the Jezebel spirit from targeting you. The bloodline is a spiritually powerful connection. She uses witchcraft, occult, divination and seduction, etc., as part of her webs to entrap people. These evil practices represent weaknesses that become the back doors of the Jezebel spirit to come into a person's life.

For example, can you imagine how the children and the grandchildren of people that had practiced witchcraft, divination, psychic, prostitution, night club stripping, (including porn stars) or even casino owners will fare when she rises up against them? They will be completely vulnerable to her. Therefore, to expel her, they will have to ask God for forgiveness for themselves and their ancestors concerning these sins. They will also have to renounce the covenants that they made with the Jezebel spirit through these evil activities before they can overcome her.

Avoid Sexual Sins

To overcome the Jezebel spirit, you must be willing to avoid sexual sins and lusts. You must not allow yourself to be enticed with sex and become entrapped in Jezebel's web. If you fail to do this, the Jezebel spirit will see your weakness in this areas and she will come in like a serpent and begin to entice and seduce you with her children or her agents. She will use them to exploit your sexual weakness in order to undermine your authority and before you know it, you are dancing to her tune as she takes control of your life. As Christians, we have to make sure that the Jezebel spirit does not control us but rather, that we are walking all over her power. If you are struggling with sexual sins always remember that you can run to the Lord for forgiveness and deliverance; His Word works.

Resist Attempts to Silence Your God-given Voice

No matter what you stand to gain, do not compromise or allow someone to keep you from speaking the Word of God. In other words, be bold and be vocal about what you believe. **Never apologize for what is written in the Bible because God's Word is the only truth that there is.** Everything outside the Word of God is a lie. We do not apologize for what God says is the truth — His Word!

Moreover, we will all give the Lord an account of what we did with His Word or His gifts that He gave us. We are not to be afraid of those who can only kill the body and nothing more. Therefore, we must walk as the Lord said in **Luke 12:4-5:**

> "And I say unto you my friends, **Be not afraid of them that kill the body, and after that have no more that they can do.** 5 But I will forewarn you whom ye shall fear: **Fear him, which after he hath killed hath power to cast into hell;** yea, I say unto you, Fear him."

Be a Strong and Effective Leader

You must be a strong, decisive and effective leader in the position that God has placed you. If you are not, she will usurp your authority as we saw with King Ahab. In her craftiness, she will send you someone who in a very subtle way undermines you and usurps your authority.

For example, have you ever heard of someone in a position of authority who trusted some new comer in the company and before they knew it, the new comer took over their job? As an agent of the Jezebel spirit, the new comer knew how to play behind the scene politics to usurp his or her boss's position. You have to recognize the authority that has been given to you and not let anyone usurp it.

Know When Dealing With the Feminist Spirit

The Jezebel spirit is a man-hater and so it works through the "feminist" groups to undermine the position of the "man in authority." Sometimes, it is a woman that is in the position of authority; in which case, the spirit uses one of the men under her to undermine her authority. Either way, she wants the position of "the Man." You can discern her agents by the way that they come against their bosses and how they do things behind his or her back. On the surface they appear friendly but behind the scene, they are nothing but serpents who cannot submit or follow instructions from the leader.

Avoid Being Pressured to Make a Decision

Some agents of the Jezebel spirit might begin to put the leader in a position to make a critical decision without giving the leader time to think about the decision. They do this to make the leader look bad, to make themselves look good to their higher superiors and to take advantage of the leader. **We will all do well to remember how King Darius made a hasting decision to enact a law that later bound him to his words and to the point that he had to give permission for Daniel whom he loved to be cast into the den of lions.** It was not his will or desire to have Daniel punished but because of his hasty decision, there was nothing that he could do but have his beloved Daniel cast into the den of lions — **Daniel 6:1-17:**

"It <u>pleased Darius</u> to set over the kingdom an hundred and twenty princes, which should be over the whole kingdom; 2 <u>And over these three presidents; of whom Daniel was first: that the princes might give accounts unto them, and the king should have no damage.</u> 3 **Then this Daniel was preferred above the presidents and princes, because an excellent spirit was in him; and the king thought to set him over the whole realm.** 4 Then the presidents and princes sought to find occasion against Daniel concerning the kingdom; but they could find none occasion nor fault; forasmuch as he was faithful, neither was there any error or fault found in him.

5 <u>Then said these men, We shall not find any occasion against this Daniel, except we find it against him concerning the law of his God.</u> 6 Then these presidents and princes assembled together to the king, and said thus unto him, King Darius, live forever. 7 <u>All the presidents of the kingdom, the governors, and the princes, the counsellors, and the captains, have consulted together to establish a royal statute, and to make a firm decree, that whosoever shall ask a petition of any God or man for thirty days, save of thee, O king, he shall be cast into the den of lions.</u> 8 **Now, O king, establish the decree, and sign the writing, that it be not changed, according to the law of the Medes and Persians, which altereth not.**

9 **Wherefore king Darius signed the writing and the decree...**<u>Then these men assembled, and found Daniel praying and making supplication before his God.</u> 12 Then they came near, and spake before the king concerning the king's decree; <u>Hast thou not signed a decree, that every man that shall ask a petition of any God or man within thirty days, save of thee, O king, shall be cast into the den of lions?</u> **The king answered**

and said, The thing is true, according to the law of the Medes and Persians, which altereth not. 13 <u>Then answered they and said before the king, That Daniel, which is of the children of the captivity of Judah, regardeth not thee, O king, nor the decree that thou hast signed, but maketh his petition three times a day</u>.

14 Then the king, when he heard these words, was sore displeased with himself, and set his heart on Daniel to deliver him: and he laboured till the going down of the sun to deliver him. 15 <u>Then these men assembled unto the king, and said unto the king, Know, O king, that the law of the Medes and Persians is, That no decree nor statute which the king establisheth may be changed.</u> **16 Then the king commanded, and they brought Daniel, and cast him into the den of lions. Now the king spake and said unto Daniel, Thy God whom thou servest continually, he will deliver thee.** 17 And a stone was brought, and laid upon the mouth of the den; and the king sealed it with his own signet, and with the signet of his lords; that the purpose might not be changed concerning Daniel."

What happened in the case of Daniel is a great lesson to any leader not to be pressured into making a hasty decision. All who are wise will learn from it because as a leader, you are going to give someone an answer that is a NO. Therefore have a policy of thinking about your impending decisions. I had manager who used to say, *"Whenever you hear an idea, never say yes right away; go to lunch and think about it. If when you come back from lunch or the next day it still sounds like a good idea, then pick it up and act upon it."*

Joseph Overcame the Jezebel Spirit

Although he was cast into the dungeon for years, Joseph stood up against the Jezebel spirit by rejecting her advances through Potihpar's wife. **Since Joseph resisted and overcame the Jezebel spirit, it means that we can overcome her too.** It does not means that it will be an easy ride but we cannot fall into her ways; neither can we afford to let her influence us or make us ignore God's Word (the fear of the Lord). When you know and live by God's Word, then you will fear Him. It was the fear of God (God's Word) that kept Joseph from accepting a life of adultery with Potihpar's wife as we see in **Genesis 39:7-20:**

"And it came to pass after these things, that his master's wife cast her eyes upon Joseph; and she said, **Lie with me.** *8* **But he refused, and said unto his master's wife, Behold, my master wotteth not what is with me in the house, and he hath committed all that he hath to my hand;** *9* There is none greater in this house than I; neither hath he kept back anything from me but thee, because thou art his wife: **how then can I do this great wickedness, and** sin against God?

10 And it came to pass, as she spake to Joseph day by day, that he hearkened not unto her, to lie by her, or to be with her. *11* **And it came to pass about this time, that Joseph went into the house to do his business; and there was none of the men of the house there within.** *12* **And she caught him by his garment, saying, Lie with me: and he left his garment in her hand, and fled, and got him out.** *13* And it came to pass, when she saw that he had left his garment in her hand, and was fled forth,

14 That she called unto the men of her house, and spake unto them, saying, See, he hath brought in an Hebrew unto us to mock us; he came in unto me to lie with me, and I cried with a loud voice: *15* And it came to pass, when he heard that I lifted up my voice and cried, that he left his garment with me, and fled, and got him out. *16* **And she laid up his garment by her, until his lord came home.**

17 <u>And she spake unto him according to these words, saying,</u> **The Hebrew servant, which thou hast brought unto us, came in unto me to mock me:** *18* And it came to pass, as I lifted up my voice and cried, that he left his garment with me, and fled out. *19* And it came to pass, when his master heard the words of his wife, which she spake unto him, saying, After this manner did thy servant to me; that his wrath was kindled. *20* And Joseph's master took him, and put him into the prison, a place where the king's prisoners were bound: and he was there in the prison"

At the end, God not only vindicated Joseph, He moved upon Pharaoh to make Joseph the Prime Minister of Egypt. He will also come to our defense when we stand up for righteousness and in due time promote us.

Chapter 12
The Jehu Anointing and Its Nature

It is the Elijah/Elisha Anointing

The anointing that destroys the Jezebel spirit is the Elijah anointing. The reason is because the Prophet Elijah was anointed by God to destroy King Ahab, his household, Jezebel, her false prophets, and her religious institutions to the idol called Baal but he received a death threat from Jezebel and he fled for his life. He was then taken up to heaven by God. As a result, he only completed part of his assignment against the Jezebel spirit because he sincerely believed that Jezebel had destroyed all the prophets of the Lord and that he was the only one left. In **1 kings 21:17-26**, we see the original commission from God against Jezebel and the house of Ahab:

> "And the word of the LORD came to **Elijah the Tishbite**, saying, *18* Arise, go down to meet Ahab king of Israel, which is in Samaria: behold, he is in the vineyard of Naboth, whither he is gone down to possess it. *19* <u>And thou shalt speak unto him, saying,</u> **Thus saith the LORD, Hast thou killed, and also taken possession? And thou shalt speak unto him, saying, Thus saith the LORD, In the place where dogs licked the blood of Naboth shall dogs lick thy blood, even thine.**

> *20* And Ahab said to Elijah, Hast thou found me, O mine enemy? **And he answered, I have found thee: because thou hast sold thyself to work evil in the sight of the LORD.** *21* <u>Behold, I will bring evil upon thee, and will take away thy posterity, and will cut off from Ahab him that pisseth against the wall, and him that is shut up and left in Israel,</u> *22* **And will make thine house like the house of**

Jeroboam the son of Nebat, and like the house
of Baasha the son of Ahijah, for the provocation
wherewith thou hast provoked me to anger, and
made Israel to sin.

23 And of Jezebel also spake the LORD, saying,
<u>The dogs shall eat Jezebel by the wall of Jezreel.</u>
24 Him that dieth of Ahab in the city the dogs
shall eat; and him that dieth in the field shall
the fowls of the air eat. 25 <u>But there was none
like unto Ahab, which did sell himself to work
wickedness in the sight of the LORD, whom
Jezebel his wife stirred up.</u> 26 And he did very
abominably in following idols, according to all
things as did the Amorites, whom the LORD cast
out before the children of Israel."

Again, from the above scriptures, we can see that the
prophet Elijah was given a mandate to judge the house of
Ahab but although Elijah was a very tough prophet with a
very fierce disposition; somehow, the Jezebel spirit got to
him and he became afraid. He asked God to take him away
to heaven and God granted his request but told him to first
anoint three people; one of whom was a man named **Jehu**
in **1 Kings 19:15-17:**

"And the LORD said unto him, Go, return on thy
way to the wilderness of Damascus: and when thou
comest, <u>anoint Hazael to be king over Syria</u>: 16 **And
Jehu the son of Nimshi shalt thou anoint to be
king over Israel:** and <u>Elisha the son of Shaphat of
Abelmeholah shalt thou anoint to be prophet in
thy room.</u> 17 **And it shall come to pass, that him
that escapeth the sword of Hazael shall Jehu
slay: and <u>him that escapeth from the sword of
Jehu shall Elisha slay</u>."

The Prophet Elijah was taken up to heaven before he could anoint Jehu so the **Prophet Elisha received the task of anointing Jehu King over Israel** in **2 Kings 9:1-10:**

"And Elisha the prophet called one of the children of the prophets, **and said unto him, Gird up thy loins, and take this box of oil in thine hand, and go to Ramothgilead:** 2 And when thou comest thither, **look out there Jehu the son of Jehoshaphat the son of Nimshi,** and go in, and make him arise up from among his brethren, and carry him to an inner chamber;

3 **Then take the box of oil, and pour it on his head, and say, Thus saith the LORD, I have anointed thee king over Israel.** <u>Then open the door, and flee, and tarry not.</u> 4 So the young man, even the young man the prophet, went to Ramothgilead. 5 And when he came, behold, **the captains of the host were sitting,** and he said, I have an errand to thee, O captain. And Jehu said, Unto which of all us? And he said, To thee, O captain.

6 And he arose, and went into the house; and he poured the oil on his head, and said unto him, **Thus saith the LORD God of Israel, I have anointed thee king over the people of the LORD, even over Israel. 7 And thou shalt smite the house of Ahab thy master, that I may avenge the blood of my servants the prophets, and the blood of all the servants of the LORD, at the hand of Jezebel.**

8 For the whole house of Ahab shall perish: and I will cut off from Ahab him that pisseth against the wall, and him that is shut up and left in Israel: 9 And I will make the house of Ahab like the house of Jeroboam the son of Nebat, and like the house

of Baasha the son of Ahijah: 10 **And the dogs shall eat Jezebel in the portion of Jezreel, and there shall be none to bury her.** <u>And he opened the door, and fled.</u>"

It is a Kingly Anointing

Jehu was anointed King over Israel. **The reason for this is because the <u>Jezebel spirit as we saw earlier is a principality</u>** *(meaning that she loves to exercise authority over nations).* **As a result, you need a higher level of authority to deal with the spirit. This was why it was necessary that Jehu be anointed King so that he could operate in that capacity.** In particular, the kingly anointing will destroy the Jezebel spirit and her institutions of witchcraft, idolatry, whoredom and all the other wickedness associated with her. **The good news for us today is that according to Revelation 1:5-6, we that are born again Christians have been made <u>Kings</u> and <u>Priests</u> unto God by the Lord Jesus:**

> "And from Jesus Christ, who is the faithful witness, and the <u>first begotten of the dead, and the prince of the kings of the earth</u>. Unto him that loved us, and washed us from our sins in his own blood, 6 **And hath made us kings and priests unto God and his Father;** to him be glory and dominion forever and ever. Amen."

<u>As a Christian, you are not going to be a **king** or a **priest** unto God in the future because you already are.</u> When you received the Lord Jesus as your Savior, you came into the position of a King and a Priest because of what the Lord did for us on Cavalry. **This is why as priests, we can offer sacrifices of praise and thanksgiving unto God with our mouth.** In this period or dispensation of grace, we do not have to kill any animal and bring the blood or make any physical sacrifices to God; the words in our mouth and the new faith in our hearts speak to God loudly.

Also, as Kings on earth and according to **Romans 5:17**, we reign and rule by the Lord Jesus Christ:

"For if by one man's offence death reigned by one; **much more they which receive abundance of grace and of the gift of righteousness shall reign in life** by one, Jesus Christ..."

We also rule on earth by His delegated authority — **Luke 9:1:**

"Then he called his twelve disciples together, and **gave them power and authority over all devils, and to cure diseases.** "

And in **Matthew 18:18-20**, He told us the following:

"Verily I say unto you, **Whatsoever ye shall bind on earth shall be bound in heaven: and whatsoever ye shall loose on earth shall be loosed in heaven.** 19 Again I say unto you, That if two of you shall agree on earth as touching anything that they shall ask, it shall be done for them of my Father which is in heaven. 20 **For where two or three are gathered together in my name, there am I in the midst of them.**"

It is an Anointing of Judgment

Once anointed, Jehu knew what he had been anointed to do and he immediately sprang into action. This is why in **2 King 9:16-27** we saw that Captain Jehu wasted no time in going to execute the judgment that he was anointed to carry out. Unfortunately for Ahaziah, King of Judah, he happened to be visiting his uncle King Joram of Israel (King Ahab's son) on the day that Captain Jehu came to execute God's judgment against the house of Ahab. Jehu killed him as well because his mother Athaliah, was Jezebel's daughter making him the grandson of King Ahab and Jezebel.

What this shows us is that the house of King Ahab in northern Israel and the ruling house of Judah in southern Israel were in cahoots together at this time because of the Jezebel bloodline. It was a major sin for King Jehoram (the son of King Jehoshaphat from the house of David) to marry Jezebel's daughter (Athaliah) thereby opening the door for the Jezebel spirit to come into the ruling house in Judah! Therefore, when Captain Jehu came to execute God's judgment against the house of Ahab, he had to kill both kings:

> **"So Jehu rode in a chariot, and went to Jezreel; for Joram lay there.** And **Ahaziah king of Judah** was come down to **see Joram.** *17* And there stood a watchman on the tower in Jezreel, and he spied the **company of Jehu** as he came and said I see a company. And Joram said, Take an horseman, and send to meet them, and let him say, Is it peace?
>
> *18* So there went one on horseback to meet him, and said, Thus saith the king, Is it peace? **And Jehu said What hast thou to do with peace? turn thee behind me.** And the watchman told, saying, The messenger came to them, but he cometh not again. *19* Then he sent out a second on horseback, which came to them, and said, Thus saith the king, Is it peace? **And Jehu answered, What hast thou to do with peace? turn thee behind me.**
>
> *20* And the watchman told, saying, He came even unto them, and cometh not again: **and the driving is like the driving of Jehu the son of Nimshi; for he driveth furiously.** *21* And Joram said, Make ready. And his chariot was made ready. **And Joram king of Israel and Ahaziah king of Judah went out, each in his chariot, and they went out against Jehu,** and met him in the portion of Naboth the Jezreelite.

22 And it came to pass, <u>when Joram saw Jehu, that he said, Is it peace, Jehu</u>? And he answered, **What peace, so long as the whoredoms of thy mother Jezebel and her witchcrafts are so many?** 23 <u>And Joram turned his hands, and fled, and said to Ahaziah, There is treachery, O Ahaziah.</u> 24 **And Jehu <u>drew a bow with his full strength,</u> and smote Jehoram between his arms, and the arrow went out at his heart, and he sunk down in his chariot.**

25 Then said Jehu to Bidkar his captain, <u>Take up, and cast him in the portion of the field of Naboth the Jezreelite</u>: **for remember how that, when I and thou rode together after Ahab his father, the LORD laid this burden upon him; 26 Surely I have seen yesterday the blood of Naboth, and the blood of his sons, saith the LORD; and I will requite thee in this plat, saith the LORD. Now therefore take and cast him into the plat of ground, according to the word of the LORD.**

27 **But when Ahaziah the king of Judah saw this, he fled by the way of the garden house. <u>And Jehu followed after him, and said, Smite him also in the chariot</u>.** And they did so at the going up to Gur, which is by Ibleam. And he fled to Megiddo, and died there..."

After killing King Joram, (Jezebel's son) along with her grandson King Ahaziah of Judah, Jehu then went in search of Jezebel herself. Queen Jezebel knew that Jehu was coming to the palace so she painted her face in her attempt to seduce him so that she can destroy him. We see this in **2 kings 9:30-31:**

"And when Jehu was come to Jezreel, <u>Jezebel heard of it; and she painted her face, and tired</u>

her head, and looked out at a window. *31* And as Jehu entered in at the gate, she said, <u>Had Zimri peace, who slew his master</u>?"

We can see from the above scripture that at the same time that she was trying to seduce Jehu, she was also belittling him by her reference to Zimri; **"Had Zimri peace, who slew his master?"** This statement was a reference to another Captain in Israel's army called Zimri who some years before the reign of King Ahab rose up against his master, King Elah, the son of King Baasha of Israel and killed him but he did not receive the support of the people. Instead, the people rose up against Zimri saying, **"A servant cannot rule in Israel."**

Therefore, all the people got together including the soldiers and they went after Zimri so when Zimri saw that not even the army was on his side, he went into the palace, burnt the palace down upon himself and died in the fire. By making the reference to Zimri, what Jezebel was saying to Captain Jehu was that when a servant rises up against his master as Zimri did previously, he does not prosper or have a peaceful ending. In other words, by invoking the treason of Zimri and how he perished, Jezebel was telling Jehu that it will not end well with him as well. **Her remarks angered Jehu** and we see his response in **2 Kings 9:32-37:**

"And he *(Jehu)* lifted up his face to the window, and said, **Who is on my side? who?** And there looked out to him two or three eunuchs. *33* **And he said, Throw her down.** <u>So they threw her down: and some of her blood was sprinkled on the wall, and on the horses</u>: **and he** *(Jehu)* **trode her under foot.** *34* And when he was come in, **he did eat and drink**, and said, Go, see now this cursed woman, and bury her: for she is a king's daughter. *35* And they went to bury her: **but they found no more of her than the skull, and the feet, and the palms of her hands.**

36 Wherefore they came again, and told him. And he said, **This is the word of the LORD, which he spake by his servant Elijah the Tishbite, saying, In the portion of Jezreel shall dogs eat the flesh of Jezebel: 37 And the carcass of Jezebel shall be as dung upon the face of the field in the portion of Jezreel; so that they shall not say, This is Jezebel."**

We see the fulfillment of God's Word over Jezebel in the above scriptures. Remember the scripture that says that we shall tread upon serpents and scorpions and that we walk over all the power of the enemy without any harm to us? **It also means that we can walk over all the power of the Jezebel spirit and it cannot harm us.** Pay attention to something that Jehu did while he was at the house of Jezebel —he ate and drank! I will talk about this later in another chapter.

It is Also Called the Jehu Anointing

The anointing that Captain Jehu received is also referred to as the **Jehu Anointing.** The reason is because God anointed Jehu King and stirred him up as His instrument of judgment against the house of Ahab and in particular against Jezebel. Therefore, this anointing **makes a person the instrument of God's judgment upon the Jezebel spirit and her idolatry.** Today, as God's kings on earth, we are uniquely qualified to go after the Jezebel spirit and to defeat her because we have already received the anointing that destroys her.

As we already saw, those that God has prepared to walk in this anointing are to reign as kings in the Kingdom of God against evil spirits. When King Ahab died, his son Jehoram became King and Jehu was a captain under both of them. Therefore, when Jehu was anointed, he became King and he was well aware of the Word of God against King Ahab and his house because he was there when the Prophet Elijah pronounced the judgment in Naboth's field.

He heard the specific judgment that God was going to bring against King Ahab and his household and **I believe that this is probably one of the reasons why God picked Jehu because he heard the judgment of God against King Ahab.** It is also the reason why after he executed God's judgment against King Ahab's son and against Jezebel, he referred to the judgment of God that the Prophet Elijah pronounced on King Ahab in **2 Kings 9:25-26:**

> "Then **said Jehu** to Bidkar his captain, Take up *(King Joram)*, and cast him in the portion of the field of Naboth the Jezreelite: <u>**for remember how that, when I and thou**</u> **rode together after Ahab his father, the LORD laid this burden upon him;** 26 **Surely I have seen yesterday the blood of Naboth, and the blood of his son** *(Jezebel killed both Naboth and his children so that there would be none left of his lineage to contend with her for Naboth's land)*, **saith the LORD; and** <u>**I will requite thee in this plat,**</u> **saith the LORD. Now therefore take and cast him into the plat of ground, according to the word of the LORD."**

It Roots Out Idolatry

This anointing rooted out Baal worship in Israel. After his destruction of Queen Jezebel, **Jehu's next move was to go after Jezebel's prophets and the whole institution of Baal worship.** He acted as a Baal worshiper and he set up a day for all Baal worshippers to come from all over the nation for a grand Baal worship but it was a trap. In **2 Kings 10:18-24,** we see how Jehu brilliantly executed God's judgment on Baal worshippers:

> "**And Jehu gathered all the people together, and said unto them, <u>Ahab served Baal a little; but Jehu shall serve him much.</u>** 19 Now therefore **call unto me all the prophets of Baal, all his servants, and all his priests; let none be wanting: for I have**

a great sacrifice to do to Baal; whosoever shall
be wanting, he shall not live. But Jehu did it in
subtilty, to the intent that he might destroy the
worshippers of Baal. 20 And Jehu said, **Proclaim a
solemn assembly for Baal.** And they proclaimed it.

21 <u>And Jehu sent through all Israel</u>: **and all the
worshippers of Baal came, so that there was not
a man left that came not.** And they came into the
house of Baal; and the house of Baal was full from
one end to another... 24 **And when they went
in to offer sacrifices and burnt offerings, Jehu
appointed fourscore men without, and said, If
any of the men whom I have brought into your
hands escape, he that letteth him go, his life shall
be for the life of him."**

Jehu had all the Baal worshippers that came to the event killed
and he actually put an end to Baal worship in Israel.

Important Keys to Remember About the Jehu Anointing

1. **It makes one God's instrument of judgment
upon all idolatry;** especially against the Jezebel
spirit. God raises up those He has prepared to walk
in this anointing to reign as kings to exercise God's
kingdom rule. For example, God sent to raise up Jehu
from among his brethren to become His Anointed
King. **Those who have this anointing have a no-
nonsense personality.** It is not everyone that can
walk in it but you should be able to recognize when
someone is operating in it.

2. **It is the anointing of <u>fierce actions</u>;** hence the
Prophet Elisha told the young prophet whom he
sent to anoint Captain Jehu to flee from the scene
after anointing him. **In other words, the fierceness**

of the Jehu anointing is such that the anointed does not waste time in springing into action right after being anointed. As we see in **2 Kings 9:2-3,** and as commanded by the Prophet Elisha, the young prophet literally ran for his life right after anointing Captain Jehu — *"And when thou comest thither, look out there Jehu the son of Jehoshaphat the son of Nimshi, and go in, and <u>make him arise up from among his brethren,</u> and carry him to an inner chamber; 3 Then take the box of oil, and pour it on his head, and say, Thus saith the LORD, I have anointed thee king over Israel. <u>Then open the door, and flee, and tarry not."</u>*

3. **It is the anointing that carries with it the mandate or command to destroy the entire house of Ahab and the Jezebel spirit without leaving any traces of them behind** —2 Kings 9: 7-9, *"And thou shalt smite the house of Ahab thy master, **that I may avenge the blood of my servants the prophets, and the blood of all the servants of the LORD, at the hand of Jezebel.** 8 For the whole house of Ahab shall perish: and I will cut off from Ahab him that pisseth against the wall, and him that is shut up and left in Israel: 9 And I will make the house of Ahab like the house of Jeroboam the son of Nebat, and like the house of Baasha the son of Ahijah."*

4. **It roots out the enemies of peace.** In other words, those who will not let peace reign in the country are eliminated by this anointing. It does not spare those who are supposed to be in God's camp but are in fellowship with the house of Ahab or the Jezebel spirit. As we saw, when Jehu found King Ahaziah of Judah with King Joram the son of Ahab, he destroyed him also. This is what Jehu said to King Joram before killing him in 2 Kings 9:22, *"***...What peace, so long as the whoredoms of thy mother Jezebel and her witchcrafts are so many?"** This anointing eliminates

the enemies of peace in the church as well as upholds the righteous standard so that those who choose a contrary way cannot stay.

5. **It is given to those who know the judgment that is written against God's enemies and who have a zeal to see it come to pass.** See 2 Kings 10:16 for the confirmation that even Jehu was aware that he had a zeal for God when he said, *"come with me and see my zeal for the Lord..."* God anointed Jehu because when he was in the garden on the day that King Ahab went to possess Naboth's vineyard, he heard God's judgment against King Ahab through the Prophet Elijah.

Even today, when the Lord sees that you have a zeal for His righteousness, He gives you this anointing because He is looking for someone who can help Him establish righteousness and Jehu was the person at that time. The Lord Jesus also had a zeal for God and it showed in everything that He did.

6. **The zeal makes you furious at the enemy.** We see the description of Jehu in **2 Kings 9:20** as follows, *"... And the driving is like the driving of Jehu the son of Nimshi; for he driveth furiously."* It makes demons flee at your presence and even before you open your mouth to speak.

7. **It makes you a sharp shooter in both the spiritual and physical realms.** You become God's expert marksman with full strength—the 2 Kings 9:24 *"And Jehu drew a bow with his full strength, and smote Jehoram between his arms, and the arrow went out at his heart, and he sunk down in his chariot."* This is similar to what David did to Goliath with the stone that he threw.

Both David and Jehu released their weapons and the anointing took over and made an impact on their targets for them. Today, we do not have to use carnal weapons because the Bible tells us in 2 Corinthians 10:3-5 that, *"Though we walk in the flesh, we do not war after the flesh: 4 (For the weapons of our warfare are not carnal, but mighty through God to the pulling down of strong holds;) 5 Casting down imaginations, and every high thing that exalteth itself against the knowledge of God ..."*

As a result, when we speak the Word, the Holy Spirit uses the Word to accomplish what we said. When I was a baby Christian, I saw God the Father in a vision sitting with a paring knife. As I watched Him, I noticed that He was very determined as He was working seriously to make an arrowhead; He was carving the arrowhead with a great zeal in order to make it more pointed and sharper. I also saw that the tree limb that He was working on was still <u>very green</u> and I knew it had to do with me. I also knew that the Lord wanted me to know that there was a chipping away taking place in my life by Him to make me a sharp shooter.

8. **It helps you carry out God's Word that is written in Ezekiel 5:11,**"*... I will not spare and neither will my eye have pity.*" Jehu did not spare King Jehoram or King Ahaziah; he followed after them and killed them. **This is one of the reasons why you do not want to be in the path of someone on a mission for God with this anointing.** If you are with God's enemies when he or she is executing God's judgment, you will go down with them because you are in the enemy's camp fraternizing with him or his agent. God judges not just workers of iniquity but also those who support acts of iniquity.

9. **It helps you find out who is really on your side and it helps you to know who is truly on God's side.** Remember that when Jehu came into King Ahab's palace, Queen Jezebel tried to seduce him by painting her face but he did not fall for it? Instead, in **2 Kings 9:32** we see Jehu asking, "Who is on my side, who?" Spiritually, this anointing will help you to identify who is really on your side and who is not; even among your so-called friends because it helps you to discern them.

10. **It gives the unspeakable joy of treading the Jezebel spirit under foot as recorded in 2 Kings 9:33,** *"...And he trod her under foot."* Jehu knew the judgment of the Lord against Jezebel and her institutions so when he accomplished the task he was anointed to do, he said in **2 Kings 9:36,** *"...This is the word of the LORD, which he spake by his servant Elijah the Tishbite, saying, In the portion of Jezreel shall dogs eat the flesh of Jezebel."*

11. **It judges all false gods.** This anointing moves the anointed to execute God's judgment on all false gods. God used Jehu to judge Baal worship in Israel and God used Moses to judge all the gods that the Egyptians worshiped such as the Nile, pharaoh, lice, frogs, cows, etc. They were all judged by the Living God.

12. **It is highly confrontational** and goes against every spirit that is a contrary spirit to the Holy Spirit. For example, see Jehu's message in **2 kings 10:1-5** to those who would rise up against him to defend the house of King Ahab:

"And Ahab had <u>seventy sons</u> in Samaria. **And Jehu wrote letters,** and sent to Samaria, **unto the rulers of Jezreel,** to the elders, and to **them that brought up Ahab's children,** saying, 2 **Now as** soon as this letter cometh to you, seeing your master's sons are with you, and there are with you chariots and horses, a fenced city also, and armour; 3 <u>Look even out the best and meetest of your master's sons, and set him on his father's throne, and fight for your master's house</u> *(Jehu was challenging them).*

4 <u>But they were exceedingly afraid, and said,</u> **Behold, two kings stood not before him: how then shall we stand?** 5 And he that was over the house, and he that was over the city, the elders also, and the bringers up of the children, sent to Jehu, saying, **We are thy servants, and will do all that thou shalt bid us; we will not make any king: do thou that which is good in thine eyes."**

This anointing is actually able to subdue those who intend to rise up against you from various spiritual levels. This is why the battle is not only on the one-on-one level with the Jezebel spirit but also with the forces that are helping to install and maintain her institutions and her doctrines.

13. **The Jehu anointing makes your "would be ad-versaries" to submit themselves unto you.** Spiritually, **as you war against the forces of darkness, you will begin to see all the devils that had been warring against you come and kneel before you in surrender.** Also, as a carrier of this anointing, there are places that you go to and even before you open your mouth, you see the evil spirits all running away as they see you coming. The first time I saw this, I was going somewhere to pray for someone and as I pulled into the parking lot, I saw the Jezebel spirit with her little children. Before I could open my mouth to speak, she began gathering her

children and running off with them. They could not wait to run out of that place because of the presence of the anointing upon me.

At other times, I would see evil spirits jumping out through the windows before I even make an entrance into a building. They are afraid of the presence of the Holy Spirit that we carry in us into the places that they had previously occupied. Sometimes, I see the devils throw their hands up in the air in surrender and run off! Some of them will wash their hands of the case and immediately surrender as soon as I open my mouth. Still, God's judgment must be carried out on them. It is the awesome grace of God to show us the victory as we war!

14. **It gives you the enemy's head in a basket.** The Jezebel spirit seeks the head of God's people but God anoints us to take off her head and since we do not war against flesh and blood (people), we take off the heads of the evil spirits. Remember that Jehu told them that they should set one of Ahab's children on the throne and fight for the house of their master? Their reply was that they were not going to fight with him but surrender to him and become his servants. He then requested the heads of all of King Ahab's children; all seventy of them — **2 Kings 10:6-9:**

> *"Then he wrote a letter the **second time** to them, saying, If ye be mine, and if ye will hearken unto my voice, take ye the heads of the men your master's sons, and come to me to Jezreel by tomorrow this time. Now the king's sons, being seventy persons, were with the great men of the city, which brought them up. 7 And it came to pass, when the letter came to them, that they took the king's sons, and slew seventy persons, and put their heads in baskets, and sent him them to Jezreel.*

8 And there came a messenger, and told him, saying, **They have brought the heads of the king's sons. And he said, Lay ye them in two heaps at the entering in of the gate until the morning.** *9 And it came to pass in the morning, that he went out, and stood, and said to all the people, Ye be righteous: behold, I conspired against my master, and slew him: but who slew all these?"*

15. **Nothing will be left of the enemy in every area that you go to root him out.** For example, it is recorded in **2 Kings 10:11** that *"...Jehu slew all that remained of the house of Ahab in Jezreel, and all his great men, his kinfolks and his priests, until he left him none remaining."* Jehu was able to totally root out Jezebel because of the anointing that was upon him. In other words, it was not by might, it was not by power but by the Spirit of the Lord.

16. **The anointing also endues you with wisdom on how to remove idolatry or idol worship.** A Good example is in **2 Kings 10:21-25** which shows us how Jehu wittingly got all Baal worshipers and priests to come to him. *"And Jehu sent through all Israel: and all the worshippers of Baal came, so that there was not a man left that came not... And they smote them with the edge of the sword ..."*

17. **It helps you get the job done!** This is written in **2 Kings 10:28** concerning Jehu, *"Thus Jehu destroyed Baal out of Israel."* As popular as Baal worship was in Israel, God raised up Jehu to completely destroy it out of Israel. As believers in the Lord Jesus Christ, we have the Holy Spirit to also help us accomplish our God-given assignments against this spirit that is bent on perverting and destroying humanity.

Chapter 13
Pitfalls of Walking in the Anti-Jezebel Spirit Anointing

I am writing about the pitfalls of walking contrary to God's Word when you have the Jehu anointing because it is only fair that if you are going to root out the Jezebel spirit that you also know these pitfalls. In order to walk successfully in this anointing, you have to avoid the things that might make you fall or ensnare you along the way. Here are a few of them.

Lack of Sanctification

This anointing calls for sanctification and all those who will walk in the **"Jehu Anointing"** must sanctify themselves.

To be **sanctified means:**
   1. To be set apart for sacred use; consecrate.
   2. To make holy; purify.
   3. Abstinence from sin
   4. To give religious sanction to, as with an oath or vow

We can say that sanctification means to set be set apart by the Lord for His use and we also have to set ourselves apart for His use as well. **It also requires that we make holy decisions and purify ourselves by avoiding the things that defile the eyes, mind and body.** In other words, we should always do our best to keep sin and iniquities away from our lives. We cannot be like the preachers who preach the Word of God publicly but behind closed doors live contrary to it. For example, we have ministers who are running around with young girls while preaching holiness and sanctification sermons from their pulpits; some ministers are even secretly sleeping with other men's wives or other men. God calls all of them hypocrites.

Not only does God see them, the devil also sees them as nothing but hypocrites; Christians that love his ways. When he is ready to bring them down, he will use their hypocrisy as a door to come against them. He usually makes a public spectacle of them because he wants to give them a permanent stain that they can never blot out in their reputation. **This is why I tell people that your ministry is based on your reputation and if you play around and ruin your reputation, only uninformed people will want to sit under you.** If they insist on remaining under you, their friends will begin to ask them what they are doing still sitting under a hypocrite. Therefore, you have to make sure that you really sanctify yourself by doing what you preach.

When God gives someone this particular anointing, failure to sanctify one's self will make the person to fall by the very hand of the Jezebel spirit. This is why you read in the papers or news media that some of the very ministers of God who are known to publicly go after her while secretly living or "swimming in her pool of ungodliness" have been exposed openly and shamefully. There are three very good examples of people chosen by God who did not sanctify themselves and as a result, fell into the very sins that they had eradicated or were disobedient and were killed. They are **King Saul,** the **young prophet** and **Jehu** whose sad endings are narrated below.

Disobedience to God's Instructions

Obedience is a prerequisite to walking successfully in the Jehu anointing. King Saul was chosen by God and for a season, he was zealous for God and as a result, he destroyed one of the Jezebel spirits' chief institutions — witchcraft! When he later sinned against God and God refused to answer his prayers or speak to him, he fell into the very witchcraft practice that he had personally helped to destroy — **1 Samuel 28:5-25:**

> "And <u>when Saul saw the host of the Philistines, he was afraid, and his heart greatly trembled</u>. *6* **And**

when Saul enquired of the LORD, the LORD answered him not, neither by dreams, nor by Urim, nor by prophets. *7* Then said Saul unto his servants, **Seek me a woman that hath a familiar spirit, that I may go to her, and enquire of her.** And his servants said to him, **Behold, there is a woman that hath a familiar spirit at Endor.**

8 And Saul disguised himself, and put on other raiment, and he went, and two men with him, and they came to the woman by night: and he said, **I pray thee, divine unto me by the familiar spirit, and bring me him up, whom I shall name unto thee.** *9* And the woman said unto him, **Behold, thou knowest what Saul hath done, how he hath cut off those that have familiar spirits, and the wizards, out of the land: wherefore then layest thou a snare for my life, to cause me to die?**

10 **And Saul sware to her by the LORD, saying, As the LORD liveth, there shall no punishment happen to thee for this thing.** *11* Then said the woman, Whom shall I bring up unto thee? And he said, **Bring me up Samuel.** *12* And when the woman saw Samuel, she cried with a loud voice: and the woman spake to Saul, saying, Why hast thou deceived me? for thou art Saul. *13* And the king said unto her, Be not afraid: for what sawest thou? And the woman said unto Saul, **I saw gods** *(plural)* **ascending out of the earth.**

14 And he said unto her, **What form is he** *(singular)* **of?** And she said, An old man cometh up; and he is covered with a mantle. And **Saul perceived that it was Samuel**, and he stooped with his face to the ground, and bowed himself. *15* And Samuel said to Saul, **Why hast thou disquieted me, to bring** me up?... *19* **Moreover the LORD will also deliver Israel with thee into the hand of the Philistines: and tomorrow shalt thou and thy sons be with me: the LORD also shall deliver the host of Israel into the hand of the Philistines.**

20 Then Saul fell straightway all along on the earth, and was sore afraid, because of the words of Samuel: <u>And the woman had a fat calf in the house; and she hasted, and killed it, and took flour, and kneaded it, and did bake unleavened bread thereof</u>... *25* **And she brought it before Saul, and before his servants; and they did eat.** Then they rose up, and went away that night."

As we see in **1 Samuel 31:6-10** below, King Saul died for his disobedience and for returning to the practice of witchcraft which he once helped to destroy from Israel:

"**So Saul died, and his three sons, and his armour-bearer, and all his men, that same day together.** *7* And when the men of Israel that were on the other side of the valley, and they that were on the other side Jordan, saw that the men of Israel fled, and that Saul and his sons were dead, they forsook the cities, and fled; and the Philistines came and dwelt in them.

8 And it came to pass on the morrow, when the Philistines came to strip the slain, that they found Saul and his three sons fallen in mount Gilboa. *9* **And they cut off his head, and stripped off his armour, and sent into the land of the Philistines round about, to publish it in the house of their idols, and among the people.** *10* And they put his armour in the house of Ashtaroth: and they fastened his body to the wall of Bethshan."

The Disobedience of the Young Prophet

There was a young prophet that disobeyed the instructions that he received from God and he ate and drank in the place that God sent him to pronounce His judgment. His disobedience cost him his life and we are to learn from it. This happened during the reign of King Jeorboam. When Solomon died, his son Rehoboam became king but during King Rehoboam's reign, God divided the twelve tribes of Israel and gave ten tribes to Jeroboam to rule over and left the house of David with two tribes. The problem was that **when Jeroboam became King, he set up idol worship in Bethel in order to keep the people from returning to the house of David by going to the Temple in Jerusalem to worship.** As a result, Bethel became the idol worship center and the people went there to worship idols instead of worshipping God at the Temple in Jerusalem.

One day, God sent a young prophet from Judah to Bethel to pronounce His judgment against King Jeroboam while he was offering his sacrifices to the idol gods. According to this Word of the Lord, God was going to raise up a child and his name will be called Josiah and when he becomes king in Israel, he will destroy the alters that Jeroboam had setup in Bethel. Jeroboam stretched forth his hand to take hold of the prophet and his hand immediately became paralyzed. He asked the young prophet to entreat the Lord for him that his hand will be restored. The young prophet prayed for him and God restored his hand — **1 Kings 13:1-6:**

> "And, behold, there came a man of God out of Judah by the word of the LORD unto Bethel: and Jeroboam stood by the altar to burn incense. 2 **And he cried against the altar in the word of the LORD, and said, O altar, altar, thus saith the LORD; Behold, a child shall be born unto the house of David, Josiah by name; and upon thee shall he offer the**

priests of the high places that burn incense upon thee, and men's bones shall be burnt upon thee. 3 And he gave a sign the same day, saying, <u>This is the sign which the LORD hath spoken; Behold, the altar shall be rent, and the ashes that are upon it shall be poured out.</u>

4 **And it came to pass, when king Jeroboam heard the saying of the man of God, which had cried against the altar in Bethel, that he put forth his hand from the altar, saying, Lay hold on him. And his hand, which he put forth against him, dried up, so that he could not pull it in again to him.** 5 <u>The altar also was rent, and the ashes poured out from the altar, according to the sign which the man of God had given by the word of the LORD.</u> 6 And the king answered and said unto the man of God, **Intreat now the face of the LORD thy God, and pray for me, that my hand may be restored me again. And the man of God besought the LORD, and the king's hand was restored him again , and became as it was before."**

To show his gratitude, King Jeroboam invited the young prophet to his house for dinner but he declined the invitation. Later that day, while he was sitting under a tree instead of getting out of the city, an <u>older prophet</u> came to him and told him that <u>an angel</u> told him to bring the young prophet back to his house to eat and drink. The young prophet **disobeyed** the Word of God and **obeyed the deceitful words** (contrary words from an angel) spoken to him by the old prophet as we see **1 Kings 13:7-26:**

"<u>And the king said unto the man of God, Come home with me, and refresh thyself, and I will give thee a reward.</u> 8 And **the man of God said unto the king, If thou wilt give me half thine house, <u>I will not go in with thee, neither will I eat bread nor</u>**

drink water in this place: *9* **For so was it charged me by the word of the LORD, saying, Eat no bread, nor drink water, nor turn again by the same way that thou camest.** *10* So he went another way, and returned not by the way that he came to Bethel.

11 Now there dwelt **an old prophet in Bethel**; and **his sons came and told him all the works that the man of God had done that day in Bethel: the words which he had spoken unto the king, them they told also to their father.** *12* And their father said unto them, What way went he? For his sons had seen what way the man of God went, which came from Judah. *13* And he said unto his sons, Saddle me the ass. So they saddled him the ass: and he rode thereon, *14* And went after the man of God, **and found him sitting under an oak**: and he said unto him, Art thou the man of God that camest from Judah? And he said, I am.

15 Then he said unto him, Come home with me, and eat bread. *16* And he said, I may not return with thee, nor go in with thee: neither will I eat bread nor drink water with thee in this place *(in the place of idolatry, God says destroy everything)*: *17* **For it was said to me by the word of the LORD, Thou shalt eat no bread nor drink water there, nor turn again to go by the way that thou camest.** *18* He said unto him, I am a prophet also as thou art; and **an angel spake unto me by the word of the LORD,** saying, Bring him back with thee into thine house, that he may eat bread and drink water *(this is contrary to the instructions that God gave him).* **But he lied unto him.**

19 **So he went back with him, and did eat bread in his house, and drank water.** *20* And it came to pass, as they sat at the table, that the word of the LORD came unto the prophet that brought him back *(the old prophet):* 21 And he cried unto the man of God that came from Judah, saying, **Thus saith the LORD, Forasmuch as thou hast disobeyed the mouth of the LORD, and hast not kept the commandment which the LORD thy God commanded thee, 22 But camest back, and hast eaten bread and drunk water in the place, of the which the LORD did say to thee, Eat no bread, and drink no water; thy carcass shall not come unto the sepulchre of thy fathers.**

23 And it came to pass, after he had eaten bread, and after he had drunk, that he saddled for him the ass, to wit, for the prophet whom he had brought back. 24 **And when he was gone, a lion met him by the way, and slew him: and his carcass was cast in the way, and the ass stood by it, the lion also stood by the carcass** *(even the lion was send as an instrument of judgment).* 25 And, behold, men passed by, and saw the carcass cast in the way, and the lion standing by the carcass: and they came and told it in the city where the old prophet dwelt.

26 **And when the prophet that brought him back from the way heard thereof, he said, It is the man of God, who was disobedient unto the word of the LORD: therefore the LORD hath delivered him unto the lion, which hath torn him, and slain him, according to the word of the LORD, which he spake unto him."**

What do you make of this kind of story where your enemy is not out there in the world but in the house of God? This incident is to let us know that those who are before us in ministry can set themselves up to destroy us or prevent us from going forward in our ministries if they perceive that we are doing what they cannot do. **This is why in your ministry, you will encounter ministers who have been in ministry for many years but have not been able to demonstrate the power of God and when they see God's power flowing through you, they might set themselves up against you.**

Therefore, you have to be careful of the counsel and instructions that you receive concerning an assignment because it is best to follow the instructions that you were given by the Lord. If you read the end of the story about the young and the old prophets, you will see that at the point of his death, the old prophet requested from his sons that they bury him in the same sepulcher where the young prophet was buried. Truly when he died, his sons buried him in the sepulcher of the young prophet. **This proved that he was coveting the anointing of the young prophet.**

The old prophet wanted to destroy the young prophet by purposely lying to him to make him to disobey God but the young prophet did not know it. The important lesson for us in this historical account is that when God sends us to judge, we have to follow His precise instructions because if the young prophet had followed God's instructions, the old prophet would not have been able to destroy him. **The old prophet was covetous, envious and jealous of the young prophet's anointing.**

The reason was because according to the report that the old prophet received from his sons, the young prophet breezed into town, demonstrated the power of God and showed King Jeroboam that there was a True God in Israel. The old prophet had been in the same city for years but had not been able to demonstrate God's power so he set out to destroy the young prophet by claiming to have heard from an angel in order to cause him to disobey God and fall. This is why the Apostle Paul said the following in **Galatians 1:8:**

> "But though <u>we, or an angel from heaven,</u> preach <u>any other gospel</u> unto you <u>than that which we have preached unto you, let him be accursed.</u>"

Even the old prophet said that the young prophet died because he was disobedient to the instructions that he received from God. Never trade the Word of the Lord for any other person's word because if you mess up, God judges you just as He did everyone else that He used to judge idolatry that messed up.

Perverseness of Jehu's Character and Ways

You cannot have perverseness of character when you receive the Jehu anointing. **We are to learn from Jehu's errors because he entered into the house of Jezebel and he ate and drank in the house that God said was ungodly and was to be destroyed.** In other words, he did not see that the place was unclean from God's perspective and it was after he had finished enjoying himself that he said, *"Go and see now this cursed woman and bury her for she is the king's daughter."*

> "And when he *(Jehu)* **was come in, he did eat and drink,** and said, Go, see now this cursed woman, and bury her: for she is a king's daughter. 35 And they went to bury her: but they found no more of her than the skull, and the feet, and the palms of her hands... (2 Kings 9:34-35)."

In the very house that he was sent to destroy, Jehu sat down to eat and to drink. In so doing, he forgot that he was dealing with a very wicked spirit that was out to destroy him. **When God sends you to destroy something in a place, do you go to enjoy yourself in that place?** By the time he was ready to see what happened to Jezebel after enjoying himself, the dogs had finished eating Jezebel except for her skull, feet, palms and hands. **What this shows us is that there was a flaw in Jehu's character.**

What Jehu was not aware of was that he was now the King and that he was the Lord's anointed. He also did not know that the anointing that empowered him to kill Jezebel actually came directly through the Prophet Elijah who would not have spent a minute in Jezebel's house. Just like the Prophet Elijah, Jehu was to fiercely enforce God's judgment without fraternizing with the enemy. Also, as the Lord's anointed, he did not know the power of his words; he was unaware that his words would later ensnare him into Baal worship. He basically made a covenant with the spirit of Baal to worship him as we see in his statement in **2 Kings 10:18:**

> "And Jehu gathered all the people together, and said unto them, **Ahab** served Baal a **little;** but **Jehu shall serve him much.**"

Also, before King Jehu gave the order for the worshippers of Baal to be destroyed, he made another blunder —**he himself offered sacrifice to Baal!** He did not see his offering of sacrifice to Baal as a covenant with the Jezebel spirit and the Baal spirit. Because Jehu was profane, he did not learn to stay away or to discern between that which is holy and that which is unholy —**2 King 10:25-28:**

> "**And it came to pass, as soon as he** *(Jehu)* **had made an end of offering the burnt offering** *(worshipping Baal)*, **that Jehu said to the guard and to the captains, Go in, and slay them; let none come forth.** And they smote them with the edge of the sword; and the guard and the captains cast them out, and went to the city of the house of Baal. *26* And they brought forth the images out of the house of Baal, and burned them. *27* And they brake down the image of Baal, and brake down the house of Baal, and made it a draught house unto this day. *28* **Thus Jehu destroyed Baal out of Israel.**"

He did not see anything wrong with himself as the servant of God offering a sacrifice to Baal and as a result, during his reign as King, he fell into Baal worship. **In other words, during his zeal for God, Jehu destroyed Jezebel and the house of Ahab but because he did not put a difference between the clean and the unclean in his life, he later fell into the very idolatry and witchcraft that he had previously destroyed.** This is why you have to be careful not to have any type of compromise with the Jezebel spirit in your character and your ways while executing God's judgment against her. What we see is that there was a serious flaw in Jehu's character and it later led to his downfall — **2 Kings 10:29-31:**

> "Howbeit **from the sins of Jeroboam the son of Nebat, who made Israel to sin, Jehu departed not from after them, to wit, the golden calves that were in Bethel, and that were in Dan...** *31* <u>But Jehu took no heed to walk in the law of the LORD God of Israel with all his heart</u>: **for he departed not from the sins of Jeroboam** *(worshipping idols at Bethel),* **which made Israel to sin."**

It is a very sad ending because Jehu who had single handedly eradicated Jezebel and her institutions of Baal worship *(idolatry)*, sexual perversion *(whoredom)*, seduction, witchcrafts, sorcery, etc., later fell into Baal worship himself. Again, when you look at Jehu's ways, there was a serious perverseness or profaneness in him yet, he was an instrument that God used to judge the people that needed to be judged except that God turned around and judged him as well.

This is one of the reasons why we always have to bear in mind that just because God is using a person to judge others does not mean that the person is immune from being judged by God. The Apostle Paul was very aware of this aspect of God's righteous standard of judgment hence he said the following in **1 Corinthians 9:27:**

"But I keep under my body, and bring it into subjection: **lest that by any means, when I have preached to others, I myself should be a castaway.**"

He knew that with great anointing, comes great responsibility. The Bible requires all those who will live godly to sanctify themselves and you must also learn to endure persecution while saying no to ungodly things. It is natural for the ungodly to think that you are strange and to say unpleasant things to you because you are not going into the ungodly places that they go into. But remember that God will be pleased with you for sanctifying yourself for Him. The truth of the matter is that due to the anointing of God upon your life, you must be different from the ungodly.

Always remember that one of the reasons that the accounts of what happened to Judge Samson, King Saul and Captain Jehu are in the Bible is for us to learn from their mistakes. Each one of them was personally chosen and anointed by God and they all failed in their calling and with each one of them, it was a character issue. The flaw in their character's made them to set aside the Word of God and it also blinded them from seeing that they were throwing away the great call that was upon their lives.

Do Not Censor God's Word

You cannot censor the Word of God in order to choose what you like about it and what to discard. You have to obey the entire Word of God without leaving out the part that you do not like. This is necessary because if you are going to execute God's judgment against rebels, you had better be obedient lest you yourself be judged as a rebel. When God judges His servants, He does it publicly so that others can learn or take heed from it. This is why the Lord told us in **Luke 6:41-42** to first take the beam out of our eyes and to judge ourselves so that God's judgment is not poured out upon us for others to learn from:

"And why beholdest thou the <u>mote</u> that is in thy brother's eye, but perceivest not the <u>beam</u> that is in thine own eye? 42 Either how canst thou say to thy brother, Brother, let me pull out the mote that is in thine eye, when thou thyself beholdest not the beam that is in thine own eye? **Thou hypocrite, cast out first the beam out of thine own eye, and then shalt thou see clearly to pull out the mote that is in thy brother's eye.**"

Avoid Idolatry and Witchcraft

Since we are now Kings and Priests unto God, He can give anyone of us the Jehu Anointing as He dispatches us against the Jezebel spirit but we have to avoid the sin of idolatry. Witchcraft and idolatry go hand-in-hand because the practice of one usually involves the other but the Holy Spirit helps us to avoid both witchcraft and idolatry because God judges those who practice them. God also hates us creating personal idols; some people's idols are their jobs, material possessions, money, fame, children, spouse, etc. Therefore, come out from these things so that you are not counted as an idolater. **The Jehu Anointing is an awesome anointing and it is one to be desired by every Christian but it carries with it some great responsibilities and as we saw, it requires true sanctification and obedience!**

Because this particular anointing is for judgment, God uses us to judge others but we have to make sure that God has no cause to judge us concerning the sins of the Jezebel spirit. **This is one of the reasons why the Lord Jesus said in John 14:30 that "the prince of this world cometh, and he has nothing in me." We also had better make sure that the Jezebel spirit has nothing in us when we are going after her and her institutions.** We all must make sure that we have a way of checking ourselves so that the perverseness that brought the judgment of God upon Jehu and that made Samson to come short of the call of God upon his life is not found in us.

Another reason to do this is because the Jezebel spirit believes in revenge and retaliation. **Jehu's house was judged because he would not stay away from going to Bethel to worship the golden calves.** In **Luke 12:47,** the Lord said that he that know to do right and does not do it shall be beaten with many stripes:

> "**And that servant, <u>which knew his lord's will, and prepared not himself, neither did according to his will, shall be beaten with many stripes</u>.**"

Failure to Watch Your Words

When you are given the Jehu Anointing, you are also given the opportunity to know the value of your words. We saw how Jehu's words opened the door for the Jezebel spirit to drag him into idolatry. Our negative words can represent powerful covenants that the devil uses against us. This is why the Bible says in **Proverbs 6:2:**

> "**Thou art snared with the words of thy mouth,** thou art taken with the words of thy mouth."

Therefore, if you are going to be God's instrument to judge others, you must constantly watch your words and make sure that you are truly sanctified to God at all times lest God brings His judgment against you also.

Summary of How Not to be Snared by the Jezebel Spirit:

- **Have an active prayer life** so that you can hear God's voice clearly

- **Walk in obedience to God's instructions to you** (*avoid the mistake of the young prophet*).

- **Do not censor God's Word by disregarding what you do not like in His Word.**

- **Recognize the Anointing upon your life.**

- **Avoid all of the Jezebel spirit's seductions** to thirst for power, recognition, prestige and the love of money. Also, do not touch God's glory.

- **Avoid her whoredoms** or sexual sins.

- **Walk in integrity** because the Jezebel spirit will exploit any lack of integrity on your part. In other words, **practice what you preach.** You have seen many preachers fall as a result of this.

- **Let there be no perverseness in your character.**

- **Be a decisive leader** – the Jezebel spirit loves leaders that she can easily entrap. She is attracted to weak leaders.

- **Avoid her traps to pull you back to your past evil ways** *(Be careful of ministering in places where you were once vulnerable).*

- **Avoid involvement in witchcraft and idolatry.**

- **Do not fraternize with her or her agents.** Be quick to recognize her and her agents and do not be like Samson who played around with Delilah.

- **Recognize those who are jealous of you and stay away from them** *(The young prophet failed to do this and as a result, the old prophet purposely destroyed him).*

Conclusion

As you have seen from reading this book, the Jezebel spirit is heathenistic in nature and has no restraints, no moral principles and no fear of God or man. **It fights against the Word of God with atheism, sexual perversions and promiscuity, homosexual doctrines, evolution doctrines, and other false doctrines. It preaches that 'everyone can determine what is morally right or wrong for him or herself outside of the Word of God'.** It is one of the main spirits that are at work in all those who are against the teachings of the Word of God as outlined in the Bible. Those who do not want to subject themselves to the Word of God love the workings of this evil spirit.

This **spirit** works through **government leaders, judicial systems, educational systems, influential members of societies (famous people included), and those close to any leader. Her goal is to subvert the general beliefs of any given society so that her doctrines can become the prevalent and the acceptable doctrines of the land.** This is why many societies are <u>now adopting</u> her doctrines and are also <u>trying to force other societies and nations to accept them as legal, moral and normal ways of **modern** life</u>. For example, homosexuality used to be regarded as an abomination by most societies because the Word of God says so but today, this spirit is fighting to have it accepted as a "civil right."

You have to guard yourself against the workings of this spirit so that it does not hinder you or cause you to fall into her web of sins. Also, you do not want to give the Jezebel spirit a reentry into your life after you have pulled her down. The Lord said that when you cast out an unclean spirit, it goes around looking for rest and if it cannot find any, it then tries to make a come-back to where it was cast out of. We are all to discern the Jezebel spirit and to stay away from her. If you have been delivered from her, please stay delivered! God bless you.

— **Prophetess Mary J. Ogenaarekhua, PhD**

About the Author

I am a born again Christian who believes in the preservation of human life and the sanctity of marriage as defined by the Bible. I also believe in letting God set our agenda rather than us setting the agenda for Him. Below is the biographical information about me.

Biographical Information

Name: Prophetess Mary J. Ogenaarekhua, PhD (pronounced **Oge-nah-re-qua**).

Founder: Mary J. Ministries, Inc.; To His Glory Publishing Company, Inc.

Educational Background: BA in Communications-Journalism, Masters Degree in Public Administration and a PhD in Theology

Dr. Mary Justina Ogenaarekhua was born in Nigeria. She grew up in a Muslim home with her grandparents and she attended Roman Catholic elementary and high schools. The Lord miraculously raised Mary up from the dead when she took a fatal fall in her early years. Prophetess Mary is gifted with the ability to heal the sick, to interpret visions and dreams, to hear the voice of the Lord, to discern spirits and to intercede as a mighty prayer warrior. She is also the Lord's scribe.

Dr. Mary operates in the gift of prophecy with the ability to see into the spiritual realm. God has opened Prophetess Mary's spiritual eyes to see His desire for His people. She's a teacher of the unadulterated Word of God; a true woman of God in rare spiritual form! She holds workshops and conferences as well as teaches and preaches on many topics including **deliverance, healing, visions and dreams, spiritual discernment, understanding the power of covenants, effective prayers, mentoring, leadership training and much more**. She conducts **evangelism and outdoor crusades internationally** with thousands in attendance.

Dr. Mary Justina Ogenaarekhua is the author of the following books:

(1) Unveiling the God-Mother. This book is a biography of *Mary's death and resurrection experience* and her early years in Africa. It details the spiritual events that happened to her before she became a Christian and before she came to the United States. She also discusses some of the events and holidays that a lot of Christians celebrate ignorantly.

(2) Keys to Understanding Your Visions and Dreams: A Classroom Approach. In this book about visions and dreams, she uses the Word of God to instruct the body of Christ on visions and dreams. She applies the first-hand revelation knowledge that she learned from the Lord Himself. This book is a must read for everyone who dreams and everyone who sees visions. It will teach you how to interpret both with the Word of God.

(3) A Teacher's Manual on Visions and Dreams. This manual is designed to teach the average person, bishops, pastors, etc., the basic principles about visions and dreams, about sources of vision and dreams, about identifying the sources of your visions and dreams and about analyzing their contents. It is meant to be used along with the above textbook titled, *Keys to Understanding Your Visions and Dreams*.

(4) How to Discern and Expel Evil Spirits. This is a very powerful book for all those who are called to the healing and deliverance ministry. In it, Dr. Mary answers the questions most people have concerning evil spirits, and she teaches on the origin of evil spirits, how to discern and expel them and she answers the question, "Can a Christian have a demon?" This is a foundational resource for all those who want to walk in great spiritual discernment and to cast out devils.

(5) A Teacher's Manual on Discerning and Expelling Evil Spirits. This is a powerful teacher's tool with a step by step teaching on key principles about evil spirits, the origin of evil spirits and how to identify and expel evil spirits. It is meant to be used along with the above textbook on *How to Discern and Expel Evil Spirits*. If your desire is to teach others, you can follow the teaching strategies outlined in this book.

(6) How I Heard from God: The Power of Personal Prophesy. Prophetess Mary Ogenaarekhua outlines key principles concerning personal prophecy and she lays out a blue print of what to do with your personal prophetic words. She helps the reader understand <u>the conditions that are attached</u> by God to every personal prophetic word. Failure to understand these conditions will keep your God-given prophetic word from coming to pass.

(7) Effective Prayers for Various Situations: Volumes I and II. In *Effective Prayers,* Prophetess Mary outlines principles on how to pray effectively concerning various life situations. <u>Both of these books contain prayers for almost every situation that a lot of Christians battle with</u>. Many have given testimonies about the deliverance and blessings manifested in their lives as a result of praying the prayers in these books.

(8) Keys to Successful Mentoring Relationships. In this book, Dr. Mary outlines the dynamics involved in a mentoring relationship and the actual steps and stages of mentoring. She also highlights the pitfalls to avoid.

(9) A Workbook for Successful Mentoring. This workbook is a powerful teaching guide for all those who want to be mentored and those who desire to mentor others. It is a teacher/student's valuable tool for teaching and practicing mentoring. It is meant to be used along with the above textbook titled, **Keys to Successful Mentoring Relationships**.

(10) Understanding the Power of Covenants. This book teaches on the power of covenants. Covenants impact our lives for good or for bad on a daily basis. It allows us to learn about how God uses covenants, how the devil uses covenants and how God wants us to use covenants so that we can receive what He has for us and avoid the devil's attempts to use negative covenants to hinder us. Negative covenants can hinder a person's progress throughout the person's life.

(11) Secrets About Writing and Publishing Your Book: What Other Publishers Will Not Tell You. This book is a powerful synopsis of what you need to know in order to write and get your book published and also how to position your book for mass marketing. It is designed to help all those who desire to write and market their books.

(12) The Agenda of the Few. This book is a call for the Church to get back to its God-given purpose for this country (USA); which is to reach <u>all</u> Americans for God. For too long now, <u>the Church</u> has been functioning as though it is only called to one political party –the Republican Party. The issues discussed in this book are meant to remind the reader that there are Ten Commandments in the Bible and that God can choose to address any of these commandments at any given time. Therefore, we must be willing to get the Church out of the Republican Party box that we have placed it in and learn to seek God's will during each presidential election. He is God of the Republicans, the Democrats and the Independents.

(13) The Agenda of the Masses. Just like the *"Agenda of the Few"* above that was written to the Christian Conservatives in the Republican Party, this book addresses what the Lord showed me that a lot of the <u>Christians in the Democratic Party</u> are doing that equally displeases Him. They have allowed a very large segment of the Church to be pulled away by "the agenda of the masses." In other words, they have bought into the ungodly doctrines, ideologies, beliefs, and political views of the masses to the point that now, their version of Christianity within the Democratic Party is essentially "anything goes." In their attempt <u>to please the masses</u>, they have embraced the pagan gods and have lumped their worship together with the worship of the Judeo-Christian God of the Bible.

(14) What Tribe of Israel Am I From? This book is designed to answer the questions of some Christians who are trying to determine the tribe of the <u>natural Israel</u> that they are from. The reason they want to know this is because there are some teachings going on in Christendom in which Christians are being assigned to the various tribes of Israel. This book will help anyone to determine the tribe of Israel that they are from. It is an eye-opener for anyone who desires to know the truth.

(15) Experiencing the Depths of God the Father. This book is the first in a series of three books titled, *Experiencing the Depths of God the Father, Experiencing the Depths of Jesus Christ,* and *Experiencing the Depths of the Holy Spirit.* It is written to help you know God in depth as well as understand the mysteries that He has coded in His Word for you. Therefore, this book is for you if you want to know God in a deeper way so that you can receive all that He has for you. It is truly a book for all those who want to know God in a deeper more intimate way.

(16) Experiencing the Depths of Jesus Christ. This book is written to help you know Jesus in depth and to know how <u>He existed in the spiritual realm</u> as well as <u>in the Old Testament</u> before He was manifested as the <u>Son of God</u> on earth. It is filled with revelation of who the Lord Jesus is and how He has been dealing with us since man fell into sin. You will be excited as you see the Lord Jesus revealed to you in a way that you have never known before.

(17) Experiencing the Depths of the Holy Spirit. God the Father and the Lord Jesus are both in heaven; it is the Holy Spirit that is here with us on earth and both the Father and the Lord Jesus relate to us through the Holy Spirit. Therefore, we need to get to know Him better so that we can learn His ways and be better able to follow His leading and guidance. This book is written to help you know Him in depths.

Dr. Mary O. lives in Atlanta and is the founder of **Mary J. Ministries** and **To His Glory Publishing Company, Inc.** She is an ordained minister with a strong Deliverance Anointing. She has appeared on Trinity Broadcasting Network and other national television programs.

About Mary J. Ministries

Mary J. Ministries was founded by Dr. Mary J. Ogenaarekhua to equip and impart the anointing of God to the Body of Christ, for the purpose of impacting the whole world. Our goal is to help men, women, old and young to build relationships through Bible Studies, Community Outreach, Prayer Support, Caring Ministries, Teaching on Visions and Dreams, Discernment/Deliverance, Evangelism, Mentoring, Fellowship and Special Events.

As an ordained minister, Prophetess Mary O. teaches, trains and activates individuals to properly operate their prophetic gifts, discernment, deliverance and ministry outreach and interpretation of visions and dreams. Teachings provided by Prophetess Mary O. are inspired by God and are balanced biblical principles for the purpose of developing a spirit of excellence, wholeness and GODLY character.

Prophetess Mary O. is committed to helping the Body of Christ and those who do not yet know the Lord Jesus as their personal Savior to understand their God-given purpose. Mary J. Ministries regularly hosts classes, seminars, conferences and crusades in this nation as well as in other countries.

Mary J. Ministries
Phone: **770-458-7947**
Website: www.maryjministries.org

About To His Glory Publishing Co.

To His Glory Publishing Company, Inc. was also founded by
Dr. Mary J. Ogenaarekhua to help writers become published
authors. Our goal is to help new and established writers edit,
publish and market their work for a reasonable cost.

To His Glory Publishing Company, Inc. offers one of
the most cost effective and stress- free ways of getting a
manuscript published.

Books published by To His Glory Publishing Company will
be made available in most of the major on-line bookstores like
Amazon.com, Barnes & Noble.com, Books-a-million.com, etc.

**Our authors receive a 40% royalty on the net sales of their
books!** Upon request, we submit our published books for
buyers and distributors such as Wal-Mart, Family Christian
Bookstores, drugstores, Publix and Kroger for review and
purchase for their chains of stores.

**We are a Christian organization with the sole purpose of
bringing glory to the name of our Lord Jesus Christ.
Therefore, we will not publish obscene or offensive materials.**

To His Glory Publishing Company, Inc. reserves the right to
reject any manuscript it deems obscene or offensive.

To His Glory Publishing Company, Inc.
Phone: **770-458-7947**
Website: www.tohisglorypublishing.com

Bibliography

Josephus, Flavius. *Antiquities of the Jews,* Book 8, Chapter 13:19 (pages 316-317).

Ogenaarekhua, Mary J. *Unveiling the God-mother.* Atlanta, GA: To His Glory Publishing Company, Inc., 2004.

Ogenaarekhua, Mary J. *Understanding the Power of Covenants.* Atlanta, GA: To His Glory Publishing Company, Inc., 2008.

Rouillé, Guillaume. *Promptuarii Iconum Insigniorum.* Lyon, France: 1553.

To His Glory Publishing

Let Us Publish Your Book

To His Glory Publishing Company will publish your book at the least expensive cost. We pay one of the highest royalties in the industry – 40%! We print on demand and place your book on the major online bookstores such a Amazon.com, Barnesandnoble.com, Bookamillion.com, etc.

TO HIS GLORY PUBLISHING COMPANY, INC.

463 Dogwood Dr. Lilburn, GA. 30047, U.S.A (770)458-7947

Order Form for Bookstores in the USA

Order Date: _____

Order Placed By: _____   By Fax: _____

Address: _____

_____

City _____ ST/ZIP _____

Phone #: _____

Email: _____

Purchase Order#: _____

Return Policy: Within 1 year but not before 90 Days.

Price	Quantity	List Price
Shipping Method:		
Media:		
UPS:		
FedEx:		
Other (Please Secify):		
Total Price:	**Total Quantity:**	**List Price**

Ship To Address: **Bill to Address:**

TO HIS GLORY PUBLISHING COMPANY, INC. • 463 Dogwood Dr. Lilburn, GA. 30047, U.S.A (770)458-7947

Other Books by Prophetess Mary Ogenaarekhua

Understanding the Power of
COVENANTS

Dr. Mary J. Ogenaarekhua

ISBN 978-0-9791566-8-7

ISBN 978-0-9821900-2-9

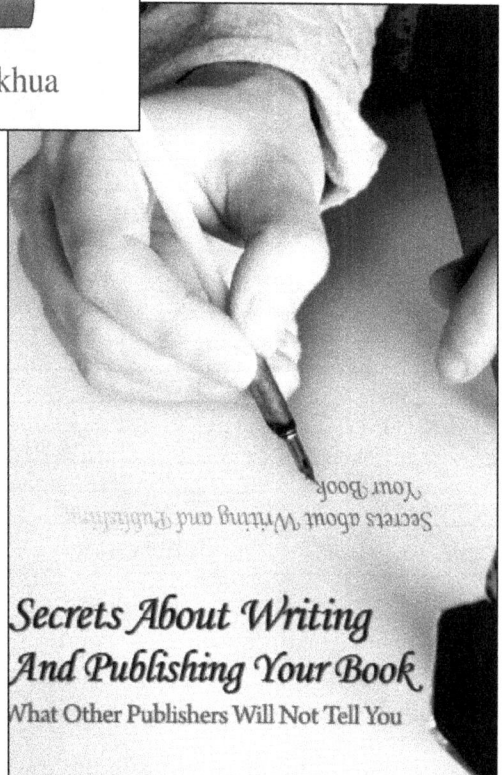

Secrets About Writing
And Publishing Your Book
What Other Publishers Will Not Tell You

Other Books by Prophetess Mary Ogenaarekhua

EFFECTIVE PRAYERS
FOR VARIOUS SITUATIONS

Prophetess
Mary J. Ogenaarekhua
AUTHOR OF UNVEILING THE GOD-MOTHER

ISBN 978-0-9774265-6-0

ECTIVE PRAYERS
VARIOUS SITUATIONS
Vol. II

Prophetess
Mary J. Ogenaarekhua
AUTHOR OF UNVEILING THE GOD-MOTHER

ISBN 978-0-9774265-9-1

Other Books by Prophetess Mary Ogenaarekhua

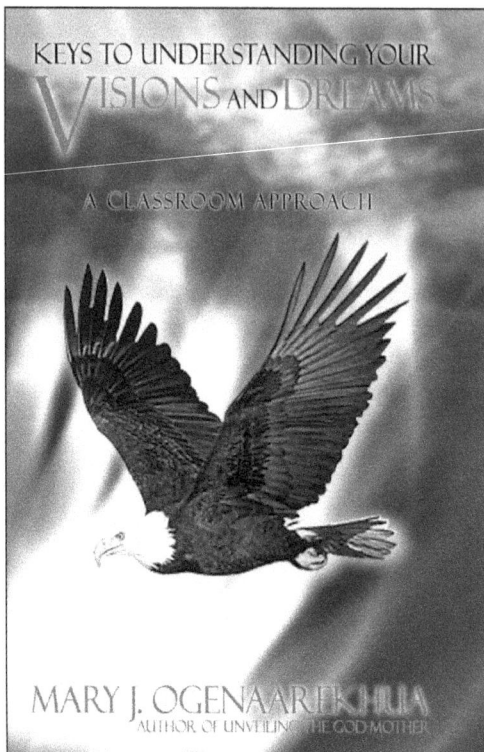

KEYS TO UNDERSTANDING YOUR
VISIONS AND DREAMS

A CLASSROOM APPROACH

MARY J. OGENAAREKHUA
AUTHOR OF UNVEILING THE GOD-MOTHER

ISBN 978-0-9749802-1-8

ISBN 978-0-9749802-8-7

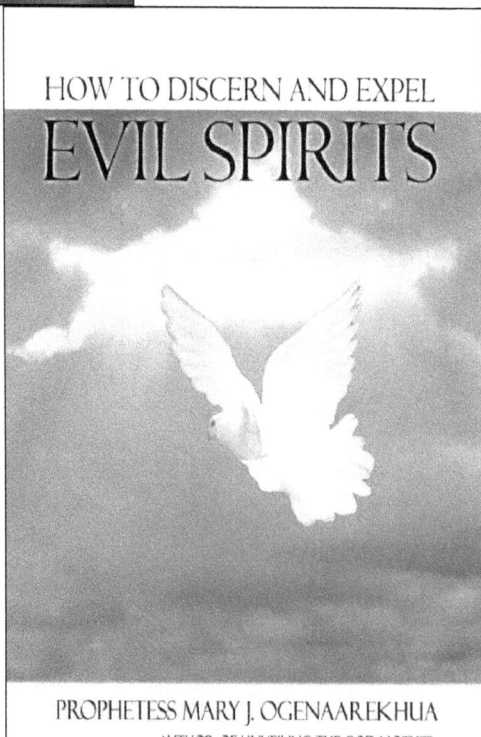

HOW TO DISCERN AND EXPEL
EVIL SPIRITS

PROPHETESS MARY J. OGENAAREKHUA
AUTHOR OF UNVEILING THE GOD-MOTHER

Other Books by Prophetess Mary Ogenaarekhua

ISBN 978-0-9791566-6-3

ISBN 978-1-5873628-0-4

ISBN 978-1-5873628-0-4

Other Books by Prophetess Mary Ogenaarekhua

ISBN 978-0-9821900-1-2

ISBN 978-0-9821900-4-3

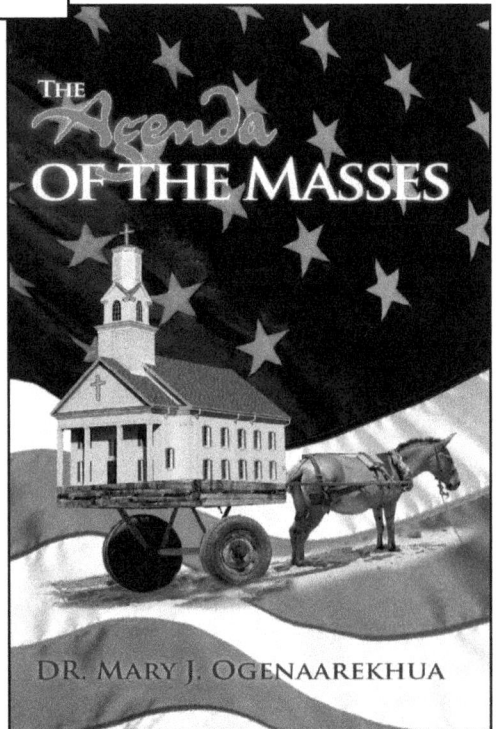

Other Books by Prophetess Mary Ogenaarekhua

ISBN 978-0-9821900-7-4

ISBN 978-0-9821900-8-1

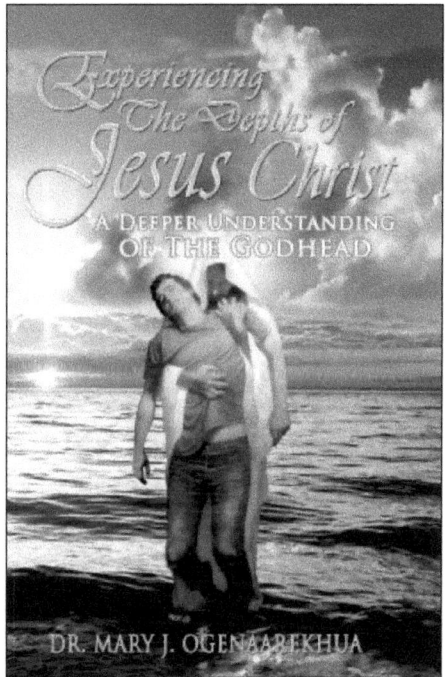

ISBN 978-0-9854992-2-8

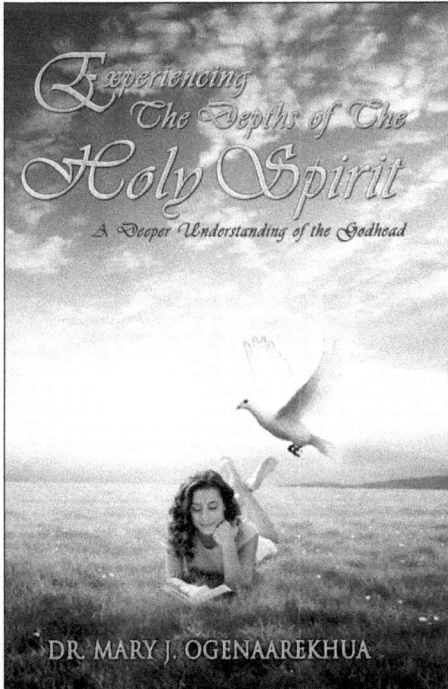

www.ingramcontent.com/pod-product-compliance
Lightning Source LLC
Chambersburg PA
CBHW072104080426
42733CB00010B/2201